Trouble

Personal Story Publishing Project Series

Bearing Up, 2018
- making do, bearing up, and overcoming adversity

Exploring, 2019
- discoveries, challenges, and adventures

That Southern Thing, 2020
- living, loving, laughing, loathing, leaving the South

Luck and Opportunity, sping 2021
- between if and if only

Other selected titles by Randell Jones

Scoundrels, Rogues, and Heroes of the Old North State, 2004 & 2007
by Dr. H.G. Jones, edited by Randell Jones & Caitlin Jones

Before They Were Heroes at King's Mountain, 2011

A Guide to the Overmountain Victory National Historic Trail, 2011,
second edition, 2016

The American Spirit, 1780, 2016 (free YouTube video)
(link from www.danielboonefootsteps.com)

From Time to Time in North Carolina, 2017

Available through Daniel Boone Footsteps
www.danielboonefootsteps.com
1959 N. Peace Haven Rd., #105
Winston-Salem, NC 27106

Trouble

Randell Jones, editor

Daniel Boone Footsteps
Winston-Salem, North Carolina

Daniel Boone Footsteps
1959 N. Peace Haven Rd., #105
Winston-Salem, NC 27106

RandellJones.com
DanielBooneFootsteps.com
DBooneFootsteps@gmail.com

Scars are like tattoos,
just with better stories.
— various origins

Preface

This book is the fifth in a series of anthologies, collections of personal stories on a set theme, our Personal Story Publishing Project. We began in 2018 with *Bearing Up*, a collection of 45 stories on the theme of "making do, bearing up, and overcoming adversity." For *Exploring*, in 2019, our writers shared stories of "discoveries, challenges, and adventure," again true stories from their own lives and sometimes from the lives of family members or ancestors. *That Southern Thing*, in 2020, resonates with "living, loving, laughing, loathing, leaving the South." The spring 2021 collection shares personal stories "between if and if only" under the title *Luck and Opportunity.*

The book you are holding is the result of our fifth Call for Personal Stories, this one on the theme: "*Trouble*—causing, avoiding, getting in, and getting out." It is our second collection of the calendar year and begins what we want to nurture as more opportunities for writers to get their writing out into the world. We thank the scores of writers who responded to the call by submitting such interesting, thoughtful, and well-crafted stories. They delivered the diversity and depth of perspective we were hoping for and the humor and insight which proved we chose the right theme. Each story is limited to 800 words. The writers and we have all found the Personal Story Publishing Project through its five iterations so far to be an instructive and rewarding writing experience. For the readers, it is a delight.

We received submissions from many writers in North Carolina but also from writers reaching across the country. And, we had one submission from Switzerland. We wish we could have printed them all, but we are delighted to continue sharing 45 stories in each collection.

In June 2019, we launched a second outlet for sharing the work of these fine writers with a broader audience. Their work can now be heard in our twice-weekly podcast, "6-minute Stories." Our podcast is available through Apple Podcasts (iTunes), Spotify, and Stitcher. Stories from *Trouble* will appear in the podcast's fourth season. You can listen directly to "6-minute Stories" and find all the stories archived at RandellJones.com. Episodes are announced on Facebook @6minutestories.

Trouble, the Personal Story Publishing Project, and "6-minute Stories" podcast are undertaken by author and publisher Randell Jones, doing business as Daniel Boone Footsteps in Winston-Salem, North Carolina.

Thank you for enjoying and appreciating good storytelling. And, remember...

Everybody loves a good story.[sm] •

Contents

TROUBLE

Contents

xi

Contents

xiii

Introduction

We have heard it said that if all of us took our troubles and put them on a pile to be redistributed, each of us would reclaim our own. Maybe so.

Trouble. Nobody is looking for it, but it finds us anyway. It catches us unawares or it follows us around like a shadow. When we are in the middle of it, all we can think about is getting out. And if we see it coming, it's something we'd rather step around, if we can. And if we don't, we may soon discover it's not always so easily wiped from our shoes.

Or sometimes we make trouble for ourselves or for others for one reason or another. We are the instigators and purveyors of disarray, disturbance, and dismay. If we make it for ourselves, we have only ourselves to blame. But if we are the cause of trouble for others, it's better if by accident than by intention. The former may lead to the grace of forgiveness, and the latter more likely to earn us the enmity of another, to start a revolt, or to get us a "whoopin.'" Or maybe our grandmothers were right when they said of one clueless, irritating troublemaker or another, "Small potatoes cook best in their own stew." And perhaps we do.

Trouble is an aberration, a departure from the ordinary and the expected. Trouble is expectations unmet and foiled, plans—ours or other's—gone awry from what someone had in mind. Trouble comes from not getting what we want and from wanting what we can't have. It comes from not paying attention to what and whom we should and casting our gaze in other directions when and where we shouldn't. In the end, trouble may lead to our getting exactly what we deserve—God forbid.

We were gratified by the response to our Call for Personal Stories, and we are grateful to all the writers who invested time and energy into crafting personal stories for possible inclusion in this anthology. From among the submissions, we chose stories to include based on the quality of the writing and the resonance of the personal experiences shared with the announced theme, *"Trouble*—causing, avoiding, getting in, and getting out."

Writers share early memories, some from difficult childhoods splashed with anger and moonshine and some from episodes of wholesome family life with tomfoolery inflicted and mischief survived. Stories explore the loyalty of good dogs and bad cars, the lingering of guilt, the fear of dying, and the terror of experiencing in real time the imminent possibility of unimaginable loss. We read about the struggles of choosing between parents, the blessings of care and caregiving, and about calculating sex. We read of the scamming of neighbors, animal attractions, and confronting fearsome predators—wrestling reptiles and trapping rats and "bearly" getting away. Writers share stories about getting high by accident and accidently getting by, about an elaborate cover-up at the election polls, and about aversion to a home remedy worse than the ailment. Stories explore taking stock of life worry for worry, visitations by angels or their proteges, standing naked before the world, and staring death in the face. We read of running toward and running from and racing on for racing's sake. We muse about growing and going, being left behind, and remembering those we lost. These writers uncover what they did not mean to find and find themselves at a loss for words and being misunderstood. We read stories about knowing less than we need to know and knowing it and about experiencing payback as its own reward—and punishment. Some stories have us looking back farther than we have left to see forward, seeing what was in front of us all along, and learning from other's mistakes so we don't have to make them ourselves. And as if we hadn't already discovered the timelessness of the matter ourselves, we find stories abounding about the foolishness of youth, another absolute certainty of our human experience, all of it touched from time to time by trouble.

As you will read, the stories presented here are a testament that good storytelling is alive and well. Some will make you stop to think, some to laugh out loud, and some to be grateful that you were spared anything like what others endured. Other stories will cause you to drift into your own recollections to ponder an experience of your own. We do indeed hope that your own personal stories will come to mind. We hope also that you might write them down, share them in your own circles of friends and family, and invite those folks to do the same. Personal stories connect us all in powerful ways.
Take the time to share yours. Make the time to listen to others.

Introduction

So, now you have before you a pile of trouble to sort through. You may find something close to those of your own in here somewhere. We hope you will appreciate the stories these writers lay bare for your edification and encouragement and sometimes just your entertainment. These are stories of trouble from their lives that they have tossed on the pile— some troubles for you to pick up for a moment or two, troubles to roll around in your mind and to consider.

Just remember to put them back when you're done. •

RJ

The Guilty Hat and a Traveler's Mistake

by Mary Alice Dixon

The hat was guilty, the saucy secondhand beret. I was innocent. Really, I thought I was, except for sins of fashion. Twenty years ago, on a budget trip to Paris, a hat seduced me, bringing nothing but trouble. But I made a big mistake, too.

"I intend," I had announced to my black cat Alice a week before my December get-away, "to transform myself into one of those effortlessly understated French women in their elegant black turtlenecks and just-so-scarves." Me, a Carolina girl whose birthright is primary colors, pink azalea earrings, and open-toed sandals.

"It's true, isn't it, Alice, that the French always wear black?"

Alice lifted her nose in silent disdain, a Parisienne, no doubt, in a former life.

For the 5-day trip my overpacked Samsonite included four black sweaters, three black skirts, a dozen black knee socks, and my faux-leather high-heeled boots. At the last minute, I tossed in my canary yellow ski jacket. On the "red-eye" to Paris, I sat swathed in the funereal folds of a black coat from Goodwill. The coat hem dragged around my feet but the color—and the price—were right.

I should have studied my *Fodor's French for Travelers* on the long flight, but I never opened it. My last formal brush with French had been a pass/fail college course, which I passed—just barely—decades earlier.

Arriving in Paris I took a high-priced cab to a low-priced inn. A gilt-framed poster of Madame de Pompadour hung above the bed in my tiny room. Barely glancing at the Pompadour, I headed for the Eiffel Tower, *Fodor's French* in my hand, still unopened.

Crossing a filigree platform half-way up the Tower, my coat hem caught in the fancy ironwork. I tripped, falling on my fanny. Francs spilled from my pockets, ricocheting through latticed levels below.

"Watch it, lady," an American teenager yelled.

After tripping again, unhurt though humiliated, I left the Eiffel Tower to wander the Latin Quarter, browsing for a coat that fit. No luck. But a black velvet beret called to me from a vendor's vintage clothing cart. Picking up the used hat, I thought I inhaled old perfume.

"A hat with a past," I said, smitten.

Placing the beret on my blonde head, I became Bergman in *Casablanca*. The hat was mine.

The next morning, dressing for a day trip to Chartres, I set the beret at a jaunty angle, playing coquette in a mirror.

TROUBLE

"I'll wear my true colors," I told the Pompadour poster, pulling on my neon yellow jacket and high-heeled boots. The Pompadour looked down at me, inscrutable in her sepia smile.

Several hours later, entering Chartres Cathedral, I found a Mass in progress. A stooped sexton ushered me to a seat as if he expected me. Several white-haired women turned, staring at me. All wore black.

Feeling conspicuous in my beret, canary jacket, and high-heel boots, but being a cradle Catholic, I tried to follow the service but could not understand a word. Soon I rose to join a Communion line. But when I reached the altar, I discovered I was actually in a receiving line for a funeral.

In front of me a tall French matron wept quietly beside a coffin. The officiating priest stood next to her, blessing each mourner who came before him. Fearful of being rude, I stayed, hoping to pass unnoticed.

The priest's shoulders jerked when he saw me.

"*Bonjour*, Father," was all I could muster, although a "good day" it was not. He stiffened. I bowed my head. Off fell the hat, landing right at the widow's feet.

She gasped, pointed at me, wailing.

"*La maîtresse, la maîtresse.* (The mistress, the mistress)."

The funeral stopped, all eyes upon me. I froze. I wanted to explain I was just a tourist, had never met the dead man, that this was a terrible mistake. *Fodor's French for Travelers* failed and so did I.

The Guilty Hat and a Traveler's Mistake

"Excusez-moi," I said, which means "Excuse me" but also means "Forgive me." Even to me, my words sounded confessional.

"La maîtresse, la maîtresse," she shrieked.

Heart pounding, I picked up the fallen hat, wondering if the widow smelled another woman's perfume. Then, despite my high-heeled boots—and I'm not proud of this—I ran down the nave and out of the cathedral, a streak of yellow in a sea of black.

I did not mean to be callous, but I was young and silly. On the train leaving Chartres, I whispered to the hat, "Oh well, we'll always have Paris." The guilty hat stayed silent. I never wore it again.

I never fully understood the widow's mistake. For years I blamed the hat for all the trouble. But the real mistake, a traveler's mistake, was mine: I should have studied the French before I went to France. •

Mary Alice Dixon lives in Charlotte, NC, where she is hospice volunteer, retired professor, former attorney and happy member of Charlotte Writers Club and Charlotte Lit. Her recent work is in *That Southern Thing, Belmont Story Review, Broad River Review, County Lines, Kakalak, Fourth River, Main Street Rag, moonShine Review, North Dakota Quarterly, Passager's Pandemic Diaries, Pinesong: Awards 2021,* and elsewhere. You can sometimes find her daydreaming with an old copy of *Fodor's French for Travelers* in her lap and a black hat on her head.

An Encounter Beyond the Boundaries

by Janice Luckey

One afternoon, stifling humidity laid to waste all good intentions. With sweat pooling under our eyes, my older brother and I rode our bikes in front of our house on Alfred Street. The St. Augustine neighborhood, thick with pointed palmettos and Spanish Moss-draped live oaks, was still. Whiffs of apricot-scented oleanders only added to the heft of the air.

We knew we were to stay near the house going no further than the length of the black steel fence surrounding the Florida School for the Deaf and the Blind. We knew the boundaries well; at least my brother knew them well. I mostly just followed wherever he went, as kid sisters often do. He tolerated me most of the time—when we played cowboys on stick horses in the back yard and when I whispered my hopes and dreams in his ear as we rocked together on the front-porch swing. But that day he pushed the boundaries and ventured off to explore where we shouldn't have. Even at my young age I knew if we were found out, Mother would shout, Dad would scowl, and sister would cry tears of empathy.

We trekked up one street and down another, each one looking identical to me. As afternoon slid into evening, he circled around to return home. Mosquitoes swarmed and emerald lizards darted across the cracks in the sidewalk. Once friendly trees became menacing giants with clutching arms; curling gray moss were strands of rope waiting to entangle lost boys and girls. And I was sure we were lost! Anxiety nattered at my stomach. Still my omnipotent brother pedaled onward. Loyally, I followed.

The dingy houses around us now were ramshackle, their yards crisp with sun-baked sandspurs. The gap between us widened as he rode on more determinedly and I lumbered to push pedals I could barely reach. Soon a shoestring of my red plaid sneaker loosened and wound itself into my bicycle chain. Grinding to a halt and balancing on one foot, I yelled for help at my brother's disappearing red cowlick. I yelled louder. Still louder. Stop! Wait! His head bobbed out of sight. How could he abandon me stuck like this?

I was stranded in front of the most dilapidated house I had ever seen. Boards hung like broken arms. Torn screens exhaled through the windows. Unruly shrubbery climbed the house like cat burglars. When a gnome of a man hobbled from the house, fear grabbed me by the throat. A gray stocking cap pulled over his inscrutable eyes framed his shriveled pecan of a face. A frizzled white beard streamed to his waist; a slender rope cinched his tattered pants. He scuttled toward me clutching something shiny in his gnarled hand. Trapped and trembling, I could only stand helplessly, one foot bound in the chain, the other riveted to the sidewalk, and wait for certain death.

TROUBLE

The sinister storybook character smelling fusty, of sweat and loneliness, said not a word, only bent down and with blunt-tipped scissors snipped my shoelace free. Before my bike could clatter to the ground, I shot down the street. Tears of both fury and relief streamed from my eyes when I spotted my dad and brother approaching in the distance.

My brother and I did pay a consequence for our disobedience that day, but there was no shouting, scowling, or crying. It was more a sorting out, a reassembling of my shattered trust. Dad held me in his arms and explained that the "scary creature" who had come to my aid was just a harmless old man that some called a hermit.

My brother's betrayal wasn't explained away as easily. I was the kid sister, he the older brother who should look out for me and keep me safe. But my brother had not heard my cries for help, Dad said with only a passing shadow of sadness on his face, because he was deaf.

Deaf? Had I known my brother was deaf? Was there a knowing inside me yet unnamed? The naming of it, the living out of it affected me in a visceral way, cleaving my childhood innocence in two. The illusion of the protected baby sister burst and I was thrust into—or did I assume?—the role of being his protector. From then on I shielded him from playground bullies, taunts on the bus, and took on anyone who called him "deaf and dumb." In an era often unkind to those with disabilities, I was his strongest ally.

That childhood tendency would evolve into a rewarding

An Encounter Beyond the Boundaries

7

25-year career as a sign-language interpreter. The brush with my bugaboo that humid afternoon so long ago turned out to be the genesis of who I became—in my family, in the world. •

Janice Luckey, who lives in Davidson, North Carolina, is a member of the Write On! writing group sponsored by her local library as well as the online writing group Impromptu. Writing became a rhythm of her life when she scribbled a romance novel in a 3-ring binder in junior high school. This sparked a life-long love of all things writerly—writing, reading, journaling and hoarding office supplies. Janice was a contributor to the 2020 and spring 2021 Personal Story Publishing Projects. You can see more of her stories at LKNConnect.com. When Janice isn't writing she can be found encouraging her four granddaughters' creativity or roaming libraries, bookstores, and Staples.

The Trouble with Mating Season
by Lisa Williams Kline

I wasn't ready to go to the beach. We needed to deal with too many things. My husband's mother, who was forgetting how to use the phone. Both of our daughters' weddings in one month—one delayed because of COVID, the other that evolved just because of love.

My husband had also been having cluster headaches. These are called "suicide headaches" because they are so severe that people commit suicide rather than endure the pain. Jeff had tried many treatments—medications, a painful nerve block—and the headaches continued. Each evening, around eight o'clock, they arrived. The anticipatory anxiety was almost worse than the headaches. And I'd be putting cold compresses on his forehead in a dark bedroom. Should we drive four hours away from his neurologist?

And need I mention our decrepit 18-year-old dog who could not be left with anyone?

Should we really just leave this behind and go to the beach?

Besides, the forecast was terrible. Rain for the entire week.

"We're going," Jeff said.

And so, a few hours later we were in the car on the way down Hwy. 74, with our ancient dog, Candi, and our cat, aptly named Lionman because of his routine sneaky bites. Most people leave their cats behind. My husband, the veterinarian, does not.

"Smell that air!" Jeff said as we crossed the bridge, rolling down the windows. "It just makes me relax."

The sun shone on the waving grasses and the gnarled yaupon trees did backbends over the road. The salty ocean breeze blew between us. The weather was gorgeous in spite of the forecast.

It just made me more tense. All the trouble we were trying to leave behind; what right did we have?

Within the hour, Jeff was ready for the beach. After a bout with melanoma, he slathers himself with sunscreen every day.

"I'll get the bed and towels ready and meet you down there," I said. I needed to decompress. As I made our bed, I wondered, *What if Jeff's headaches don't ever stop?* The neurologist was so capable and conscientious, yet to our every question—"What causes these?" or "How long does it take for them to go away?"—he would answer, "We don't know." *And Candi.* She wore diapers, she could barely walk, she had terrible cataracts and got stuck in corners. We had to take her out over a dozen times a day. How long could this go on?

The weddings were the happy part. We were crazy about our sons-in-law-to-be and the planning had been a joy. Yet there were a few worries. What about inviting this person? What about replacing that vendor?

And above all, how could we help Jeff's sister, the major caretaker, with his mother? More caretaking was needed. More visits. More talks.

Making the bed, my mind went back over my years caring for my parents, who both had dementia. The last time I saw my father. Holding my mother's hand the week before she died. How she never recovered from my father's death.

All of a sudden, out of nowhere, came a thought: *What would I do without Jeff?* That thought jolted me so, I put down the pillowcase and stared out the window at the golden waning sun, stunned.

At that moment my phone sang with a text message.
There was an alligator in the water. People came running up to tell me because I was swimming.

An alligator, during mating season, had somehow ended up in the ocean—only a dozen feet from Jeff. Another beachgoer raced to the edge, yelling, "GET OUT OF THE WATER!"

Jeff scrambled for the shore with only seconds to spare. People ran down the beach, shouting at other swimmers, like a scene from *Jaws*.

He texted again.
That guy could have saved my life.

I shook as I read his text. Was it coincidence that I thought about losing him the very moment he was near the alligator? I am not a superstitious person but sometimes things like that make me pause.

The Trouble with Mating Season

Jeff came in, visibly shaken, pale. I gave him my usual peck on the forehead, no fanfare, yet my heart was pounding in my chest. He showed me a photo from his phone of the 12-foot alligator thrashing through the surf.

We ate dinner, discussing what might have happened to the alligator. Did Wildlife Control coax him out of the ocean and back to the marsh? Did he ever find his elusive lady friend? Those things we'll never know.

Then we talked about Jeff's brush with melanoma. The weddings. Caring for his mother. And then retrieved Candi, stuck behind a door. While we were talking, Lionman bit my leg.

Life, glorious life, teems with trouble.

To our surprise, that night, Jeff's headaches were gone. •

Lisa Williams Kline has published a number of short stories and essays in various literary magazines, as well as a collection called *Take Me* (Main Street Rag). She has won the *Press 53 Fiction Open Award* and honorable mention in the *Glimmer Train Winter Fiction Open*. She's also published eleven books for young readers. She lives in Davidson, North Carolina, with her husband, who is a retired veterinarian, a cat who can open doors, and a sweet chihuahua who hardly ever barks.

A Real Doozy

by Tonya Staufer

Something felt wrong. Something was wrong. I had awakened alone in my great-grandmother's cottage located behind her main house. This wasn't how my morning was supposed to begin. Where were my parents?

The night before, my mom had tucked me in, saying, "Go to sleep now. We're going to spend tomorrow at the beach!" For me, this was the highlight of our yearly visit to Great Grand's home in Central Florida. Like most 6-year old's, I adored the ocean. I'd build my sandcastles and adorn them with colorful shells and seagull feathers. I'd gone to sleep dreaming of these pleasures.

I hurried to pull on my bathing suit, expecting to find everyone at the main house enjoying the big ol' Southern breakfast that Great Grand's cook was famous for preparing. The buttermilk biscuits with homemade strawberry jam were my favorite. What I hoped for and what I got couldn't have been more different.

Lulu, the cook, greeted the slammed screen door with, "Sweet honey, pick your breakfast cereal out and have a seat over yonder." Ignoring her and the lack of waiting biscuits, I flew into the parlor. Great Grand sat in her chair embroidering, and my grandparents on a nearby yellow chintz sofa were reading the newspaper.

"Where are Mom and Dad? Auntie Georgia and Unkie Roy? I'm all ready for the beach," I said, swinging my new bucket and shovel in the air.

"Well, honey, all the grown-ups left early for Daytona, but don't fret. We've got a lovely day planned for you," offered my smiling grandmother.

"No, that's wrong." I declared. "I'm supposed to go to the beach and build my sandcastles. I even have a new sifter for my bucket. See?"

As the summer day grew hotter, so did my anger at my wayward parents. I did have some fun playing in the pool, eating Lulu's fried peach pies until I was ready to burst, but that was no substitution for a day at the beach. I wanted revenge.

I went inside and found all three Grands. "I've been thinking. They should have woke me up and told me we weren't going today. I'm gonna pay back Mom and Dad for leaving me behind."

"You are, huh? Just what do you have in mind?" I saw my Grandpa wink at the two women.

"I'm not gonna tell y'all," I announced, "but it's a real doozy." I felt proud to be gaining the imagined upper hand, and I took my grands' nodding heads as signs of approval and understanding.

I stood outside with the afternoon sun blazing down on my head, fueling my anger even more. I'd begun to think I couldn't hold out much longer when I spotted my parent's new 1959 Oldsmobile with all the latest gadgets coming up the winding drive. Inside I could see four smiling faces directed my way. Behind my back, I held my weapon of sweet revenge. At that moment, my aunt activated one of the car's gadgets. Down came the back window. I chose to ignore her calling my name in greeting. Instead, I whipped the garden hose from behind my back, opened the nozzle full blast, and shoved it through the car window. My aunt's face received the first baptism of cold water.

I had just begun to wash away their sins when I heard my dad's voice trying to be heard over the water spray and my aunt's sputtering and coughing. "Georgia Dell put the damn window up. From the driver's seat, he yelled, "Tonya Gaye, you're in some big trouble. Shut that hose off this minute."

I turned the hose toward that voice and aimed for my new target.

A Real Doozy

"I can't find the button," my aunt wailed, trying to move the wet hair from her eyes. The water spray returned to her. Over the next brief minute, I kept the hose moving inside the car as my mom, dad, aunt, and uncle tried to escape their fates until Grandpa, who had been enjoying the show, turned off my water supply. My weapon and I had begun to tire anyway, as had my desire for revenge.

They all clambered out of the car, looking like a giant wave had washed them home. I saw the splendid success of my hosing. Unfortunately, I also could see the immediate consequences coming after me.

The next day did find me on the beach building sandcastles though sitting comfortably was a bit of trouble. Still, I would much rather have had that spanking than the dressing down my parents got from Great Grand for not telling me about their change of plans. The wages of sin, it seems, are relative. •

As an author, Tonya is moved by the effect humor and narratives have on readers. She is enthusiastic about crafting stories with beguiling characters, adding dashes of humor, and engaging dialogue that leaves her fingerprint on each page. She is published in anthologies, e-magazines, local press, and literary magazines. She is a member of Poets and Writers. Her books include *Old Mountain Cassie: The Three Lessons, A Secret Gift, Baubles to Die For,* and *Red, White, and Boom.* She writes under the pen name Tonya Penrose. Find her at www.tonyawrites.com.

Conversations with My Neighbor
by Ami Offenbacher-Ferris

Friday Morning
"Ozwald go potty. Go potty right now. Ozwald!"
Her low voice hissed through lips surrounding toothless
gums. "I said go potty. I swear I'm gonna put you in the oven
Ozwald, go potty now!" The minuscule chihuahua goes potty.

Friday Afternoon
"Does my wittle Ozzie Wazzie has a sticker in his foot?
Come here baby, mama will make it all better." Little chihuahua
disappears into an ample bosom.

Saturday Dusk
Neighbor sits precariously upon my plastic lawn chair.

"I still can't believe I weren't invited to the wedding, you know
what I mean? They didn't even ask me to go with them!
I couldn't have gone, you know what I mean, on account
of Ozwald and all but that hurt my feelings! You know what
I mean?" Neighbor squeezes chihuahua and pats his head.
Bulgy eyes look up at me imploringly.

I shake my head yes, I do and wonder what a new lawn chair will cost.

Tuesday After Rain Storm
"My sister used to fall out of bed all the time when we was little, you know what I mean? On account of we had to share a twin bed, you know what I mean? When it stormed real bad, our little brother wanted to get in the bed with us but we told him, NO BOYS ALLOWED and besides, there weren't no room, you know what I mean? That made him fire-eatin' mad. He said the first one of us to pop our head up from under the covers was going to get bashed over the head with a ball-peen hammer. My sister Annie, she poked me in the ribs and made me sit up and my brother bashed me over the head with a ball-peen hammer, you know what I mean? There was blood everywhere. I got sixteen stitches at the county hospital and boy was I mad at my sister. She drowned a couple years later in the big pond on the farm."

Maybe I should forget about replacing the lawn chair.

Tuesday Dusk
"These mosquitoes sure like you. They buzzin' all round your head. Those big ones there are the males. My brother told me when I was little that a male mosquito was the most dangerous animal on the planet, you know what I mean?"

"Those are Mayflies," I pointed out.

"Nope. Male mosquitoes. You can tell by that long dangly thing hanging down right there. You know what I mean?"
I gulped. Hard.

TROUBLE

Wednesday Afternoon

"He liked to sniff gas, my little brother. Did it his whole life from the time he was way small. You know what I mean? It's on account of my momma drank gas when she was pregnant with him. Gasoline for cars, you know what I mean? My dad said she craved it. She ate coal when she was pregnant with me. Dad had to go get some coal and break it into little pieces so she could chew on it like tobacco, you know what I mean?"

"And your other sister, Annie?" I asked.

"Annie drowned in the big pond on the farm. You know what I mean?"

Saturday Mid-morning

"Wedding didn't happen. Guess the bride went into labor the day before the wedding right during the rehearsal, you know what I mean? They're all up at the hospital with her."

I mention that I did not realize the bride was pregnant.

"Yup, groom forgot to put his raincoat on I guess, you know what I mean?"

I blinked, got it and battled with myself to keep from giggling.

Sunday Evening

"They got married early this mornin'. They could've invited me, you know what I mean, with it being delayed and all. Course, Ozwald wasn't invited and I couldn't go without him so it's fine, you know what I mean? You really should replace this chair. It could break and you'd fall right to the ground and where would you be then? You know what I mean?"

Conversations with My Neighbor

"I guess with nowhere to sit?" I hazard.

"No! You'd have to come to my place, and I got no chairs, so you'd have to sit on the floor with Ozzie, you know what I mean?" The little chihuahua growls at me. I growl back.

"Why don't you get a couple of lawn chairs for in there?" I asked.

"Don't need 'em. I got yours to sit in, you know what I mean?"

I nod and say, "Yes, I know what you mean." •

Ami Offenbacher-Ferris lives in Wilmington, North Carolina. She is a published poet through Cameron Art Museum's Writers Respond to Art Program. She was awarded the Certificate of Completion in 2021 the 24-Hour Poetry Marathon. Ami also writes short stories, creative nonfiction, and fiction. She has written two stage plays and is currently working on a book of poetry. She is a contributing member of several local and out-of-state writer groups, and stage-play and screen writers groups. She is known to her closest friends and relatives as Gypsie.

Damn Yankee?

by Joel R. Stegall

Today, when we say someone is a "Yankee" we mean a person who lives in the northeastern part of the U.S. or a player on one of New York's baseball teams.

But when I was growing up in the South in the 1940s and early '50s, to call someone a "Yankee" was an insult fraught with antebellum animosities inflamed by the Civil War and perpetuated by a self-destructive allegiance to the "Lost Cause." Adding the adjective "damn" was almost redundant. "Damn Yankee" was one word," not a joke. And you certainly would not have wanted one in your family.

With combat deaths exceeding 620,000, the conflict some diehard Southerners called the "War of Northern Aggression" brought wide-spread death and destruction on both sides. My home state of North Carolina lost 31,000 men, more than any other state, North or South, except possibly Virginia. For over a century afterward, in parts of the South, the blame for this calamity was planted firmly at the feet of the "Damn Yankees."

Heartbreak and loss were felt deeply among my ancestors.

Damn Yankee?

Historical documents confirm that three of my four great-grandfathers were among the Tar Heels who suffered or died serving in the Confederate Army. One was killed in combat near Petersburg, Virginia. Another, a guard at North Carolina's notorious Salisbury Prison, died when harshly-treated Union POWs revolted. A third was taken prisoner after the Confederates lost the Second Battle of Fort Fisher in the largest amphibious assault in military history before World War II. Tragedies of the war shrouded all branches of my family tree for at least two generations.

My fourth great-grandfather remains a mystery. I recall no stories about him. My family history research unearthed nothing except the last name, Stack. But a few hints lurked in the shadows of innocent documents and stories. Possible evidence of trouble.

What is clearly documented is that my father's mother, Grandmother Emeline Stack, was from a farm in Anson County, North Carolina, east from Charlotte. When I was a child, I remember my parents saying that during the Civil War, a unit of Maj. Gen. William Tecumseh Sherman's hated army camped out for a time on the Stack family farm. The story, they said, brought up sad memories for Grandmother Emeline. When I asked for details, Mother said only, "Bad things happened." She offered nothing more. I did not understand then. Maybe now I do.

Early in 1865, Gen. Sherman launched the Campaign of the Carolinas, one of the last Union military operations against the South. With a mission to eliminate any remnants of Southern resistance, Yankee forces marched north from Savannah to Charlotte and then turned east. Travelling on foot, accompanied by horses and wagons, the troops sustained themselves by confiscating provisions from farms on the way. As they moved through Anson County in late-February, they chose to make their camp on the Stack farm, where something happened, a story that affected Grandmother Emeline deeply.

By the time Sherman's troops occupied the Stack farm in February 1865, every able-bodied Southern male who had not already died was on active duty somewhere as the Confederacy made a final, and futile, effort to survive. It is almost certain that Sarah Stack's husband was away from home—if he had not already been killed. That left Sarah, a young woman in her early-30s, alone to look after four young children. With no evidence a husband was at home, somehow Sarah became pregnant. Given the circumstances, it seems most probable that—in the term of the times—she was ravished.

It is impossible to know exactly what happened. A senior officer may have suggested that if Sarah would cooperate, life would be easier for her and the children. More frightful and painful possibilities abound. She could have been attacked violently by one or more vengeful or drunken soldiers. As Gen. Sherman himself said, "War is hell." Whatever the details, one thing is certain: on November 23, 1865, nine months after the Union Army came through Anson County, Sarah Stack gave birth to a baby girl and named her Emeline. I have found no record that Sarah's husband ever came home. Emeline grew up without a father.

Damn Yankee?

When Emeline Stack was about 19, she met Green Stegall, a young man from a farm down the road a piece. Green had been four years old when his father, Thomas Stegall, was killed in the POW riot at the Salisbury Prison on the Friday after Thanksgiving Day, 1864. Emeline and Green married on Christmas Eve 1885. They had ten children. Their oldest boy, Frank, became my daddy.

Although my unknown great-grandfather was almost certainly a scoundrel and a rapist—and a Damn Yankee—without him I would not be here to tell this tale.

War is hell, and so can be the truth. •

Joel R. Stegall, a music professor and academic administrator, began his academic career as a choir director and then chair of the music department at Mars Hill University. He later served in administrative posts at Ithaca College, the University of Florida, and Shenandoah University. From this last post, he developed and led a Russian/American academic exchange program. Since retiring to Winston-Salem, he has worked as an academic consultant, amateur woodworker and as a not-quite-inept general household handyman. Five of Joel's stories have appeared in the Personal Story Publishing Project series.

The Massacre

by Carol A. Ford

O n Good Friday I declared a moratorium on the killing. In respect for the Christian holiday and for my peace of mind, I would not set the traps again until Easter Monday, not that the varmints would appreciate this stay of execution—or pack their bags and leave.

Ever since the extermination began, a sense of dread had settled over me, and it heightened each night as I mashed the cheese into the tiny metal plate and set the trigger, careful not to lose a finger to its quick release. Slowly with the aid of a spatula, I eased the trap into a lunch bag, which was wide-open and sitting by itself in the flour drawer. As I shut the drawer, my chest tightened. The trap would spring sometime in the night. I wondered if I would hear it. Would the creature feel it? Not that this execution was not justified—they had invaded my space, contaminated my food, and persisted until my procrastinating nature reached its limit.

I did not spring into action at the first sight of their leavings, you know, those little brown pellets that look like chocolate sprinkles, the ones that Baskin-Robbins puts on children's ice cream cones. I'd cleaned those up for weeks on the kitchen counters, the stove top, the oven drawer below the stove with its random nest of pots and pans. Even after I moved the corn meal, the flour, the rice, after I vacuumed out that drawer, they returned and left their dirty markings. Weeks went by and spring came, but they did not leave. Much like my husband's family, they stayed too long, ate too much, and failed to clean up after themselves. The trap was the only answer—for the critters, that is.

The first morning after I set the trap, I awoke to the knowledge that death was in my house, in that drawer, waiting for me—the undertaker. I lay in bed postponing the moment, but there was no peace. Forcing myself into the kitchen, I opened the drawer slightly, then a little more, just enough to see if a tail was sticking out of the bag. I gasped and shut the drawer quickly.

My husband was in the shower, unaware of the unfolding drama. I hurried to the bathroom and ripped back the curtain. "There's a dead one in the trap. I can't touch it."

"What are you talking about?" he asked, his head sporting a halo of shampoo bubbles, and his eyes open just a slit.

"The trap—it has one in it. I can see the tail. I can't touch it. You have to do something."

"Well, not right now." He ducked his head into the flow of the shower and out again. "Give me a minute."

TROUBLE

This tragedy replayed itself three mornings in a row. Each morning my husband would dispose of the body—trap and all—and then taunt me by identifying the deceased. "I think it was the mother," he said that first morning. "They're probably looking for her now." I cringed. The second day the "victim" was a fat one, he said, with a little gray in its coat. "The grandmother," he announced coldly, perhaps remembering his own granny who had never been the warm and fuzzy sort. Fortunately for me, he was late for work on the third morning. With no time for foolishness, he simply disposed of the remains, mercifully and without comment.

Easter is behind me now, and two nights have passed with no tail visible when I peep into the flour drawer. And my husband's family did not come for the weekend, another mercy, giving me two tranquil days.

As for those furry critters, how should I proceed? Do I call it quits? Have they taken flight? Did I obliterate the whole tribe? Even as I consider all of this, I am examining the stove top for tell-tale signs. I search behind the toaster oven, one of their favorite haunts. Both are clean. I ask my husband what to do. He reminds me that we are on our last trap. They come in packs of four, he says. He offers no further advice. I'll try fresh cheese, give it two more nights, and pray that the slaughter is over. I need my peace of mind. And next year when the feast of the resurrection comes around, I pray that those varmints will be no part of it. As for my in-laws, no such luck. Next year is my turn to have them. •

The Massacre

27

Carol Ford lives in Winston-Salem, North Carolina. She has enjoyed writing as a hobby for much of her adult life. Married for over 40 years, she has two sons and two grandsons. They inspire many of her stories. She signed up for community classes in creative writing in her middle years. She met like-minded folks and they eventually became a writing group meeting monthly. This is one of the stories she wrote during that time.

TROUBLE

The Strawberry Incident
by Jill Amber Chafin

Every afternoon, for the summer of 2020, my 2-year-old daughter, Poppy, indulged in a bowl of sliced strawberries. COVID-19 had ripped away all playdates, preschool, and summer camp, so the least I could do was spoil her with the sweet juiciness of her favorite fruit. From her eyes, life couldn't get any better.

Until the day a chunk lodged in her throat.

Step #1: Make sure the child is actually choking.
Signs include gagging or high-pitched sounds.

Poppy sat in her booster seat at the kitchen table, strapped in
since she had the tendency to bolt during mealtimes.
Her fingers greedily dove into the bowl of sliced strawberries;
her face dripped with sticky juice.

I tackled the dishes, briefly glancing out the window
at the remnants of a summer spent at home: a wading pool
with murky water, damp swimsuits flung over the fence,
a half-deflated beach ball. Behind me, Poppy's happy slurps
transformed into gasps and wheezes, and then coughing.

I whipped around. "Are you okay?" She had gagged on food before, but today she didn't answer.

"Poppy, are you okay?" I repeated.

Poppy responded with a sickening gurgle. *Something's wrong.* I dropped a plate, a deafening crash in the sink, and rushed to her, my frenzied heart already in my throat.

What should I do?

Step #2: Stand or kneel behind the child. Wrap your hands around the child's waist.

I'd taken multiple CPR and First Aid training courses in the past, back during my pre-mom days of running dance camps. Now, standing in front of a real life-threatening incident, the startling fear wiped my brain clean.

Flight, fight, or freeze. I froze. All that training for nothing.

The coughing continued. Poppy's eyes widened, her fists clenched, her skinny legs stiffened as her face twisted with confusion. *How could a simple snack turn into this?*

I stumbled closer. I held her water bottle to her quivering lips, hoping she'd take a sip, and everything would go back to normal. She looked through it. I shook my head, then placed the bottle down. *No, water would make it worse. Right?*

I patted her back, waiting for her voice to return. I still couldn't comprehend that this was actual *choking.* Her labored squeaks signified the movement of air; I remembered from one of my training courses that this was a good sign.

TROUBLE

Time slipped into a different domain, every second pounding out like an hour, the colors of the room swirling into a blur as Poppy's features sharpened into focus. She'd been struggling for less than a minute, and yet it felt like a year of terror.

Then her gasps weakened as if we'd been submerged, as if her lungs were filling with deathly water. The undeniable truth hit: This wasn't gagging.

Why couldn't I remember what to do?

Her eyes locked onto mine as she struggled for her next breath. I screamed for my husband.

"POPPY'S CHOKING!"

I prayed I was overreacting; that a few more raking coughs would do the trick. My husband's loud steps boomed down the hall. He shouted something, but I couldn't assimilate his words.

What would I have done if he hadn't been home?

Step #3: Grasp your fist with your other hand and position it below the chest, just above the child's navel. Press inward and upward with force.

My husband sat in the chair beside Poppy, unstrapped her, and flung her face down over his knee, like a limp rag doll. His fist slammed into her back, the steady *thwack thwack thwack* drowning out her strangled puffs of air. He pounded her with such vigor and force that I worried her body would snap in two.

I glanced at my phone on the counter. *Move! Freeze!* My limbs ached with indecision. *How long will it take the ambulance to navigate our country roads? How long can my child go without proper oxygen?* My trembling fingers gripped my phone. My husband continued the relentless attack on Poppy's back, her face tilted downward. I saw a flash of our sweet girl sprawled on the kitchen floor, blue-faced, still-lipped, and mute. I unlocked my phone. Every second mattered.

But then came silence. The slapping, the hissing breaths, the palpable panic—everything ended.

I looked. There on the floor, at my feet, lay the soggy chunk of strawberry. Poppy sat perched on my husband's lap, his hand rubbed her back—gently, now. Her eyes flickered with curiosity, and her eyebrows narrowed with displeasure.

"I'm not hungry anymore," she said.

Then she slid down and sauntered into the living room. My husband and I remained silent, for a long minute, before bursting into tears. I sobbed so hard I could not catch my breath. •

Jill Amber Chafin lives in Chapel Hill, North Carolina, where she is a member of the Durham Writers' Critique Group. She wrote her first short story when she was five years old and has written thousands of pages since then. She is currently juggling several works-in-progress, including a young adult novel, a memoir, and an almost-completed contemporary fiction novel. She works as a freelance writer and has her own blog about motherhood, health, writing, and more. This essay was inspired by Brenda Miller's "Hermit Crab" essay workshop.

I Come as a Thief

by Nikki Campo

When the bell rang on a Friday afternoon, I ran to my locker to meet Eryn. The only thing standing between us and our slumber party with girlfriends was a quick trip to procure snacks.

"Where should we go?" Eryn asked, unlocking the doors of her green Dodge Shadow in the school parking lot. "Janesville K-Mart?"

I did not know why we couldn't go to a closer store, but our favorite song, "One Headlight," was on the radio and we were in no hurry. We sang, windows down, cruising up Interstate 90.

At K-Mart, Eryn headed toward make-up rather than the snack aisle. There, she crouched down low by the Maybelline liquid foundation and motioned for me to do the same.

"Take one," she whispered, sliding the small glass bottle into her sweatshirt's front pocket. I froze. *Was she planning to steal? Was I?* I decided, implausibly, to slide a bottle into my sweatshirt's pocket, too. Just like that, 16 years of Sunday school, parental guidance, and logic came undone.

I thought I might vomit as we browsed other aisles. I glanced over my shoulder constantly. At the check-out, the cashier stared at me—or did I imagine that? We paid for our snacks and moved toward the exit. I half expected the parking lot to be ablaze, ready to engulf me in hellfire. When the automatic doors opened, we slid through them. The sun's rays shone like a spotlight on my face. The pilfered glass jar weighed 50 pounds in my hand. I clenched it so tightly it seemed my joints locked into place—a permanent Maybelline-shaped talon.

A man's voice interrupted my trance. "K-Mart Security. I think you two have failed to purchase some of your items."

Another wave of torment seized me, this time around the throat. Moments ago, I had become a thief. Now, I was caught. I pictured jail. My parents. Flames. This reckoning arrived as if by screaming freight train. When I turned to the security guard, I saw the nametag on his blue shirt: Carl. My dad's name. His face was younger than my dad's, and more stern. His hair a brown buzz cut. That's when I realized my pants were wet with my own urine.

Carl escorted us back into the store. We marched single file as if to damnation itself. I wondered who watched from the aisles. As we walked, my pants warmed, soggier by the second. By the time we got to Carl's windowless office, even my sneakers were sodden. I stood so I wouldn't soil the chairs.

TROUBLE

When I finally dared to glance down at Eryn, she was, unfathomably, laughing.

Carl called my parents first, who didn't answer. It was a huge, if temporary, relief. I took what felt like my first breath in 10 minutes. Eryn's mom came to claim us for a silent ride home.

At the slumber party that night, Eryn couldn't wait to tell our friends the story. I sat quietly in borrowed, dry clothes while a couple girls shook with laughter. Another looked as terrified as I felt. I wondered what my parents would do when they finally found out. Did Carl's request that we shop elsewhere in the future translate to my having "a record?" What had become of me?

Eryn and I stayed in touch for a decade, and she often laughed at our misdeed when we spoke. I'm haunted by the story 25 years later. It follows me into every store and whispers, "Hold your merchandise in front of you so it's obvious you're not stealing." Carl's face is with me when I shop, as is the conviction that someone may think I'm a thief. In a way, they wouldn't be wrong. Does that mean I am? Is "thief" an identity we can outgrow? Are we forever defined by our worst acts?

I don't remember feeling like I needed Eryn's approval in the store that day, but maybe I did. Maybe I wanted to step away from my good-girl persona and test the waters of rebellion. Or maybe I can blame my underdeveloped teenage brain for my impulsivity that day. Whatever the reason, my integrity collapsed.

I Come as a Thief

35

As a mother today to children who don't yet have cars, social media accounts, or fully developed prefrontal cortexes, I worry. Have I taught them that we stand to lose more than our integrity in the face of bad decisions? I hope they weigh their actions against a set of values that don't waiver in the face of pressure, privilege, or the make-up aisle at K-Mart.

Then again, I wonder if sometimes we must depart from our values (if only momentarily) to find our way back to them. •

Nikki Campo works as a writer and mother to three young children in Charlotte, North Carolina. She is a member of the Charlotte Writers' Club and Charlotte Lit. Her essays and humor have appeared in *The New York Times, The Washington Post, Good Housekeeping, Charlotte Parent Magazine, McSweeney's Internet Tendency,* and other publications. Her personal essay "Queen of Birthdays" took first prize in the Charlotte Writers' Club 2019-2020 Nonfiction contest.

The Terror Inside
by J.P. McGillicuddy

Threre safest place was outside. The other haven from
the terror was my bedroom. Either way, I spent a lot
of time hiding from my mother and tiptoeing around
my father.

My mother was a dutiful caretaker. She made sure my five
sisters and I had clean clothes, food in our bellies, brushed
our teeth, did our homework and went to bed on time. But her
personality also featured a violent temper that would blast off
so fast my sisters and I usually didn't see it coming. Once, my
mom boiled over because two of my sisters squabbled about
who would wash or dry the dishes. With her eyes ablaze, my
mother ordered all of us to line up in front of the refrigerator
to face her one-person firing squad. As she heaved dishes at us,
we ducked and dodged the projectiles smashing into shards
around us, though some did find her targets.

A toxic aspect of my mother's violence was the dread it
generated. She used this fear the way a sadistic guard might in
maintaining order in a prison. No matter who crossed her line

of intolerance, my mother would swiftly choose her prey, seemingly at random, and inflict violence in the presence of the other "inmates." This indiscriminate show of force meant any of us could become the next victim, regardless of behavior. As children, we were ill-equipped to unite in solidarity or offer solace to each other. The constant fear of her discriminatory wrath divided us. In the frightening flashes of our mother's fierce eruptions, we'd blame someone else. Each of us knew we were on our own.

As the only boy, I had a separate bedroom on the first floor of our house, while my older sisters shared two bedrooms upstairs. Due to their close proximity, my sisters were the predominant focus of my mother's ire. The fuse lighting my mother's bomb often related to messy rooms and, above all, dirty bathrooms. My mother could not abide a hair in the bathroom sink. Literally, it would make her throw up. Then she would seek revenge on the perpetrator. I can still hear my sisters each claiming the hair wasn't theirs.

Ironically, there was no spanking in our house. Instead, my mother hit us with whatever was within her reach or used her hand to slap us repeatedly from jaw to jaw. Even more than the physical pain, what I remember most is the rage on my mother's face as she rolled her tongue between front teeth bared like snarling Doberman fangs. She was only 5' 3", but quick, athletic and strong. We'd try to run away but she'd easily catch us, grabbing us by the arm with one hand while using the other one to smack us back-and-forth across the face. Her attacks sometimes left bruises and cuts, especially if she used the back of her left hand, enabling her diamond wedding ring to gouge our skin.

Although my father never laid a hand on my sisters, I was fair game for his fierce temper and ferocious fists. His beatings began when I was about 10, usually featuring him rapid-power pounding at my midsection as if he were former heavyweight boxing champ, Rocky Marciano. Meanwhile, I'd protect myself in a crouch, like the future rope-a-dope of Muhammad Ali versus George Foreman. Our final bout occurred when I was 15. By then, I'd grown physically similar to his 6-foot frame, so he'd lost the ability to overpower me. I still feared the assault for its emotional toll, but he knew I was no longer wary of the physical punishment.

Despite the terror and violence my mother and father dispensed, I believe they loved me and my siblings, and had the best intentions as parents. They simply couldn't control the rage burning inside themselves. Nevertheless, my strongest desire was to escape my parents and never return, which happened when I went away to college. In my early 20s, my parents and I settled into an undeclared détente, communicating politely on holidays, mostly by telephone. Aside from occasional visits, I lived my life largely removed from my parents, physically and emotionally. However, when my father died in his early-60s, a week before my 30th birthday, I found myself bawling like a newborn. I cried again as my mother succumbed to dementia after turning 70. In both instances, the depth of my grief surprised me. Eventually, I understood my sadness stemmed from losing forever the chance to have an adult relationship with my parents. Now that it's too late, I regret being unable to talk with them about my childhood. However, I couldn't force myself to re-live what I'd strived to erase from inside me.

I survived and got away. But I never fully escaped. •

JP McGillicuddy lives in Charlotte, North Carolina. A former magazine editor, he has authored numerous published articles spanning sports, health care and government. He also created and wrote "The Mecklenburgers," an award-winning local television program. His poetry received third-place award from Charlotte Writers Club in 2019 and appeared in Mooresville Arts "Beyond Poems and Paintings" exhibit in 2020. His stories "The White Section," and "Opportunity Named Harry" appeared in 2020 and spring 2021 Personal Story Publishing Project anthologies. He is a member of Charlotte Writers Club and NC Poetry Society.

U.S.-German Brew-haha

by Lubrina Burton

It is five months into the new millennium. It is as many months into my enlistment with the U.S. Army. In January I said good-bye to college, friends, and family back in Eastern Kentucky. Now I have no idea where I am, but it's somewhere in former East Germany.

The vernal sun sets on our supply point in the field of a German Army post in the middle of "nowhere" Europe. I return chilled and tired to the dilapidated barracks set aside just for us. I unfurl my sleeping bag onto my stained, squeaky bunk and crawl in. It is still daylight and I am unable to sleep. From my unwashed window on the third floor, I watch as some Panzer tanks navigate the narrow street below. After the tanks pass, shouts ring out from across the way.

"Hello, Soldier. American Girl," a lanky German soldier waves from an open window in his barracks. "We have beer. You come over?"

No self-respecting soldier would turn down an invitation for beer. An attempt to locate someone of higher rank so that

I might gain permission proves fruitless. Therefore I take it upon myself to go next door for Army Happy Hour. In the barracks dayroom stereo blasts techno music, one uniformed German soldier is tending bar, and others are crowded around beer garden tables. At least half a dozen of my own comrades have beaten me to the party and are holding steins full of amber lager.

Our hosts treat us as if we are their own comrades just returned from an arduous journey. They bring us pretzels, insist we get off our feet, and ensure our glasses are never empty. We swap Army stories. We exchange addresses and phone numbers. We trade pins, patches, even whole uniforms.

Halfway into the evening, the Americans are half drunk and the Germans have half their uniforms. Suddenly the music stops. All chatter halts, laughter ceases. In the doorway a hulking, middle-aged man wearing European fatigues appears.

"He's our—how do you say in English—our commander," my new German best friend, Dominik, says.

The officer's exact rank is lost in translation, but it is conveyed by the change in the atmosphere. He walks to the front of the room. Soldiers avoid eye-contact. He says something I don't understand. I can't speak German. Instead I attempt to read body language. Brows furrow. Mouths tighten. Backs stiffen.

Dominik translates; he says the commander has something to say to both the Germans and the Americans.

TROUBLE

"Oh, no," I push my beer away. In my pocket I finger my recently-acquired German Army pin. "We're dead, aren't we?"

Dominik smiles, "It will be okay." He pushes my beer back toward me.

I shake my head. "You don't know the U.S. Army."

In his native language, the commander booms out what sounds like an edict. To my Southern ears his voice sounds harsh, almost punitive. There is a pause in the stream of words only to allow his troops to reply in what I gather is their version of "Hooah. Yes, Sir."

The sound of my heart thumping in my ears drowns out all else. I close my eyes. My mind fills in the blanks. I am certain he is telling his men they will scrub latrines every night for a year since they traded their military issue. I imagine he will personally march my comrades and me back to our leaders who will put us on CQ duty forever. I brace myself for an international incident.

When I open my eyes, sitting before me on the table is a small porcelain plaque with a rendering of a Panzer and the division's coat of arms.

"What's this," I ask.
Dominik says, "It's a gift."

In English he must have dusted off just for the occasion, the commander says, "As a young soldier in the East German

U.S.-German Brew-haha

43

Army, I could have never imagined this day."

He pauses, swallows, then continues, "I never imagined
the wall coming down. I never imagined serving in a united
German military. I never imagined hosting the United States
Army as our allies in my home of East Germany. And I never
imagined having a beer with our American soldier friend."

Applause erupts, beer steins clink. I stare at the plaque.
The history stares back. As a girl, I read of Panzer divisions,
a wall dividing a country. Then I watched that divider fall,
reuniting two lands. Until now, I never imagined under the
armor of those Panzer tanks were people just like me praying
not for war, but for peace.

Behind Army humor I shield my musings, "Here's to an officer
giving us an award for drinking beer." I raise my glass. "Prost."

"To America and Germany. And beer," Dominik says.

"Hooah." •

Copyright 2021, Lubrina Burton

Lubrina Burton is a veteran of the United States Army. After the
service, she earned a degree in Psychology from Eastern Kentucky
University. She now lives with her husband and pug dog in
Lexington, Kentucky. Her short story, "Why Do Things Have To Be
So Hard," is featured in the 2020 Personal Story Publishing Project
That Southern Thing. She is currently writing her memoir about
coming of age in the military.

Fowl Play

by Stanley Winborne

Two weeks after my 6th birthday my family moved to Sanford, North Carolina, there I met Jake. He lived in a house across the street from us.

We became buddies on my first day in this place so foreign from the beach where I had lived. Jake showed me the woods behind his house. He pointed out paths, creek crossings and taught me how to find my way home.

Jake's father owned and operated the kind of 1940s grocery store where a person could pick out and buy a live chicken. The chickens displayed themselves from pens stacked up along the sidewalk in front of his store.

When a customer chose a chicken, Jake's father took it to the back of his store, where he killed, plucked, gutted, and butchered it. He wrapped it in brown butcher paper along with the neck, liver, heart, and other giblets. In a reverent manner, he then presented the package laid across his upturned palms to its purchaser.

Jake and I walked or rode our bikes to school together every day. Most days, Jake's father asked him to kill five or six

Fowl Play

chickens to have ready as soon as he opened for business. Often, I watched Jake kill chickens in the morning before school. He took care not to scare the skittish birds, and he performed this task calmly and quickly.

One bright fall day in 1949 during morning recess at St. Clair Elementary School, Jake called me to come see an enormous flock of migrating cedar waxwings. These colorful birds scratched along the margins of the school's playground as they ate the small cones from the red cedars that grew in the orange clay.

Thin, high whistles from the dense flock filled the air. Lemon yellow, red-orange, and soft gray colors flashed as the birds moved. Through rakish black masks, they watched us and drew closer together as we approached.

Without conscious purpose, I picked up a rock and threw it into the congregation. An act with no more intention than if I had pointed my finger at them. The consequences horrified me.

In the tight group, the sharp rock struck one bird on its dark head mask. Blood spurted from the wounded bird. It hopped frenetically flapping in distressed agony—unable to fly. The flock lifted as one, a cloud of frightened energy, then quiet. "Ohhh!" I cried.

A wave of self-disgust enveloped me. I felt paralyzed, speechless.

In a flash, a gaggle of girls gathered. Skinny, freckle-faced Carol Jean assessed the bloody scene. Her eyes bulged as she stared at me and shrieked, "You are in TROUBLE now!"

TROUBLE

She ran screaming toward our teacher, Miss McKoy, who sat on the school's steps, face toward the sun, eyes closed.

"Those boys are murdering birds," Carol Jean shouted in full run. She stumbled as she pointed back at me.

Jake rushed over to the bird and picked it up. He cradled it in his left hand, and then gripped its tiny head with his right and snapped it. In an instant, the bird died.

I gasped.

Jake looked at me and in a soft voice said, "We can't kill these creatures without reason. You saw them."

"I did and they were beautiful." I whispered.

"We either eat them or enjoy them for their beauty." Jake told me. "We don't kill them for fun. Otherwise, what does it mean? What would that say about us?"

Relieved by Jake's immediate and short counsel, I put my arm across his shoulder in thanks for his kindness.

Miss McKoy walked briskly to the scene, Carol Jean circling, still bellowing.

"Quiet please," the teacher said, "recess is over."

She looked at me and told me we should have a conference after lunch break. Near tears, I nodded.

Alone in the office with Miss McKoy after my difficult-to-swallow lunch, she asked, "What happened?"

Confused, I blurted my garbled account, and broke into tears.

Fowl Play

"And what did you learn?" She asked.

"That it's easier for Jake to tell when it's all right to kill something than for me," I replied.

"Good Lord, what makes you say such a thing?"

"Jake kills chickens most every morning and it's a good thing. I kill a bird and it is wrong. I didn't even mean to, but Jake does it on purpose. He told me it's OK if we eat the animals we kill, but it's wrong to kill a beautiful bird I didn't intend to eat," I said.

"Well, that seems like a useful way to understand a difficult question," Miss McKoy said, and then she cried.

She wiped both our eyes with her handkerchief, gave me a quick hug, took my hand, and led me back to our classroom.

Jake never again mentioned the incident. •

Stanley Winborne, III lives near Berea, North Carolina, on the banks of the Tar River. During the past 15 years, he lived in Mexico with his wife, Alice. He returned to North Carolina following her death in 2020. His short stories have appeared in several anthologies, and his current writing project, a novel entitled "Confessions of a False Evangelist," is near completion. Stanley writes to discover himself, and he enjoys writing songs, poetry, short stories, and novels. You may reach him via email at stanleywinborne3@gmail.com.

Thirteen Candles in the Dark

by Arlene Mandell

She was the mother-in-law from hell—she came "included with husband."

Ida Mandell was a commanding, formidable presence from "the old country." Her face was etched in perpetual frown; her jaw incapable of forming a smile or uttering the words "thank you." No one had been good enough for the son she idolized. Now, a modern, young bride was taking him away. This meant trouble, but I was up for the challenge.

Soon after the son and I married, she came for dinner; I had eagerly prepared her favorite dish. Upon arriving, she busybodied her way into the kitchen to scrutinize my groceries. She objected to just about everything, insisting I was to buy the same foods as she did, or she would not come back. Defiant, I replied that since her son liked my cooking, I was not about to change my shopping list! She haughtily announced, in that case, she would bring her own food from then on. The Yiddish word for this is "chutzpah," which

means "nerve." An awkward solution, but it worked.
I had stood my ground; more battles were to follow.

The harder I tried to please, the more she found ways to annoy me. Worst of all was "the microwave caper." This happened when she came to spend a week with us in our new home. After catering to her—night and day, hand and foot—I went out with a friend for a lunch break. Ida took revenge by putting raw eggs in the microwave and hitting the "Full Power" button.

When we returned, I knew something was amiss and headed for the kitchen. A congealed, yucky, yellow mess plastered the microwave. I had told her, emphatically, not to use it unless I was home. Ida complained she was hungry and had tried to help herself. She continued to give me grief when left alone, but I needed to escape from the house. She had me over a barrel!

One day, Ida let her guard down. She told me about growing up in a rural village somewhere on Poland's border with Eastern Europe. Her tone and expression mellowed as she reminisced about picking fruit in her father's orchard, to be sold at market. But her usual cold, hard look returned when she described how fights erupted at the border every time governments changed hands.

Men and older boys from surrounding towns came together in defense; women and children stayed home. When the fighting stopped, the women went out to search for loved ones, routinely walking over bodies of dead and wounded.

TROUBLE

One fateful day, she found her father and brother, both shot to death. "First responders" did not exist; she had to drag the bodies home herself. Her four younger sisters were too little to help; her mother was too ill. For the first time, I saw and felt the pain on Ida's face.

In September, during the week of Jewish New Year, known as Rosh Hashanah, my husband and I went to her apartment in the Grand Street projects of Lower Manhattan to stay overnight on the pullout sofa in her living room. Next day, the three of us would go to synagogue, then stroll along the walkway adjacent to the East River to cast our sins, symbolically, into the water.

Late that night, I woke up thirsting for a glass of water. On a round tray in the pitch-black kitchen, thirteen small, stubby candles arranged in a circle were glowing in the dark. In the morning, she told me they were memorial candles for her sister, brother-in-law, and their eleven children who perished in the death camps of the Holocaust. Not once had she ever spoken about them. I was shaken.

Late the following night, I returned to the kitchen to stand, mesmerized, in the light of those thirteen lost souls. Never had I felt such a searing link to my heritage as in those chilling moments in the dark, staring down at that tray of candles.

I softened after that; she softened too. I showed her how to properly operate the microwave; she ate my food without protest. I had put down my battle sword. On her more-frequent visits as she aged and grew frail, the two of us spent

Thirteen Candles in the Dark

long hours together playing cards or watching movies, or just talking.

Years later, when she was gravely ill, frightened, and sleeping fitfully, this devoutly religious woman asked if I *really* believe we get to be with our loved ones when we die. I told her since no one has come back to tell me otherwise, I believe we do. She smiled and fell into a deep sleep, passing away peacefully a few days later.

The "mother-in-law from hell" had been through her own hell. And at long last, I had made a difference in her life. •

Copyright 2021, Arlene Mandell

Arlene Mandell is an artist living in Linville, North Carolina. Her colorful portraits are displayed year-round at the Carlton Gallery in Banner Elk (www.carltongallery.com/arlenemandell). A native New Yorker, she loved teaching in Manhattan's Head Start program. Switching gears, she joined a travel magazine in Miami, Florida, where she met Captain Dan. Their permanent relocation to the Blue Ridge Mountains inspired a love of writing. Her memoirs "Eye of the Dolphin," "Artist Borne," "Gobsmacked in the Gulfstream," "Renegade Daughter," and "It Started with a Typo" appear on "6-minute Stories" podcast.

Seismic Shifts

by Wendy A. Miller

My son's first year of college ended unceremoniously on a recent Wednesday. The next morning, he went to his job handing hamburgers out a window. I thought, *Wow! He is adulting.*

It should have been a high-five parenting moment for me and my husband. But I felt queasy, like I had experienced a slight tremor, a tectonic-plate shift in our parent/child relationship that I was not ready to acknowledge. The aftershocks left me filled with dread for September.

Zachary, our only child, had the distinction of being a member of the Class of 2020, which meant the worldwide pandemic hijacked spring of his senior year—prom, graduation, and other rites of passage. But we moved on, focusing our attention on the fall when he would fly the nest by leaving for college.

Our trouble began when his university shut down its dorms and went to all online classes. It was a disappointment for us all. I wanted to wallow in sadness—get on my back, wiggle around in disappointment, like when our beagle rolled in dung. But experience reminded me that the stench of self-pity repels people, and that for many the virus foiled much more than plans. So instead, I put on my "mom jeans" and reassured Zachary he wouldn't get left behind as he watched other friends leave for college. Staying at home and attending online college was "Plan B," but good would come from it.

The school year took off with turbulence. His university is on the East Coast. We live in the Pacific time zone, which meant his 9 a.m. class started at 6 a.m. More bumps came when he didn't get his desired classes. The online experience lacked comradery. Without peer conversations, he couldn't gauge his progress which stressed him out. Plus, the pandemic limited his social activity to online video games primarily. Let's just say when we saw him around feeding times, he was moody and communicated mostly in caveman grunts.

As the year advanced, we all made strides. Zachary started a job at a local fast-food restaurant, which helped him get out of the house. His first semester grades encouraged him. But while he mastered big responsibilities, I puzzled over him getting stuck on simple tasks. He was reluctant to make doctor appointments, pick up prescriptions, and go on his own to get a haircut. It took all I could muster, but I vowed to zip my lips from commenting and rescuing. So, I vented my frustrations to my mom friends, who had similar struggles with their own college-age kids.

An article shed some light on the task-avoidance phenomenon we were experiencing. Psychologist Mark McConville, author

of *Failure to Launch*, explained the transition from adolescence
to adulthood requires a dramatic shift in identity. He said
it wasn't unusual for "transitioners" to avoid "the small
symbolic administrative tasks of adult responsibility."
He suggested it stemmed from a fear that adults wouldn't
take them seriously, so they avoided doing the task.

With me taking this to heart, instead of telling my son to make
the appointment, he and I talked through what questions
the doctor's office might ask. He felt more comfortable making
the call. Once he had success, it motivated him to tackle other
minor adult obligations. When he went to get his COVID
vaccination, I expected to go with him. His reply, "I can do it
myself," made me smile, but with a twinge of pain as
a parenting string ripped from me. As his adult identity
evolved, my role shifted from emphasis on nurturer/enforcer
to consultant/encourager.

I have cherished this bonus year with my son. We've shared
some sweet moments. When we lost power for five days
during an ice storm, our family laughed as we played a board
game by flashlight every evening—a memory we would not
have had if he were at college. When his university announced
that classes would be in-person in the fall, to my surprise,
I wasn't jumping up and down with delight.

I confided to my next-door neighbor my change in attitude
about Zachary leaving. "Maybe you've gained more than you
expected this year," she said, "and perhaps you're mourning
the thought of losing it."

Watching him grow in maturity was something I would have done from a distance if it were not for the pandemic.
The ground shake is more intense closer to the epicenter.

I will always be his mom, but it's time to shift my identity— shed the mom jeans. Buy some trendy slim, mid-rise, boot-cut jeans or maybe just a pair that fit me perfectly, match them with some heeled booties, and step out in the world as just me.

At drop-off, my husband and I will celebrate that Zachary doesn't need a push from our nest. He will enjoy the leap and soar. •

Wendy A. Miller lives in Portland, Oregon. She is a member of Taste Life Twice Writers. Her story "Mom Conquers Volcano," appeared in *Luck and Opportunity* (2021) from the Personal Story Publishing Project and featured in their 6-Minute Stories Podcast. Other work has been in *Adelaide Literary Magazine, Quail Bell Magazine,* and *Grown and Flown,* where her essay ranked 14 in their "Parent Best Posts of 2020." *Tiny Seed Literary Journal: Anthology Forest* (Aug. 3, 2021) and *The Weekly Avocet* (#450) have published her poetry. Her website is www.wendyamiller.com

Never Underestimate an Old Man

by Carlton Clayton

We did not expect the old man to have a gun. When he fired it, I dropped my ice cream cone. I don't know if he fired it at us or into the ground or into the night air. All I know is that when we rounded the corner of the Tastee-Freez, he knocked open the door and yelled, "STOP!" We mocked him and laughed as we ran past. That's when he fired the gun. It sounded like someone whacking a sheet of roofing tin with a hammer.

The old man worked the evening shift at the Tastee-Freez in James City, North Carolina. He was as plain as anything could be in his black pants and white, long-sleeve shirt. He was maybe 65 or so, tall, and as skinny as a bean pole, and had white, wiry hair. His black-framed glasses had thick magnifying lenses that gave him big bug eyes. Jeffrey and I, barely teenagers, had our baseball caps pulled down to partially cover our faces that hot summer night in 1971. We decided the old man would be the best one to dupe since he wouldn't be as quick on his feet as the two much younger employees.

We were wrong.

He chased us into the pecan orchard where we split up. Jeffrey ran toward the railroad tracks at the northwest side. I ran toward the road at the east edge, stopped just short of it, and hid behind one of the tall pecan trees. It was quiet in the orchard, and it felt as if we were in a game of hide-and-seek. I wondered where Jeffrey was, and I was sorry for getting him into this mess.

Short, rapid breaths. I peeked around the tree and saw the old man's glasses as he stood stock-still against the tree my mother and I favored when we picked pecans together in the fall; the lights at the gas station behind him lit up his lenses like a flare and cast the side of his face in a silhouette. I could see his nose jutting out below his glasses like a dowel. And I could see the outline of the gun, the barrel pointing up to the black sky, ready to take aim. We were less than 50 feet apart. He could not move because he knew we'd discover his location if he rustled the brush beneath his feet. I was locked down for the same reason.

I felt a fear I'd never had before, and, at the same time, I experienced a rush that made this sudden risk of life an awesome juvenile adventure.

I wanted to run for it. It was only four or five steps to the road and the darkness beyond, and since several trees stood between the old man and me, he wouldn't have a clear shot—but I did misjudge his agility. I wondered how many bullets he had left. He fired off two rounds, I'd thought, but I couldn't remember. It all sounded like one big blast. I couldn't take that chance of running off, not solely because of my own safety but Jeffrey's safety, too, and I couldn't leave without him because I was responsible for the cockamamie situation we were in. The whole ice cream take-and-run idea was all mine.

I was snug against the tree. The dry, gaping bark smelled like worn shoe leather and was as rough against my face as cracked asphalt. I tasted the ice cream on my tongue—vanilla, chocolate-dipped—though I didn't remember ever taking a lick. Then I heard the old man's footsteps crushing leaves and snapping twigs. The footsteps got louder, it seemed, and my body stiffened against the tree as I dug my fingers deep into the channeled bark, my eyes squeezed shut. Warm pee poured down my legs into my Cracker Jack tennis shoes.

The footsteps trailed off, and it was quiet again in the orchard except for the buzz of the traffic along the road. I opened my eyes and peeked around the tree. The old man was at the back door of the Tastee-Freez. He stopped, jerked around, and looked back into the orchard as if he had heard something. I thought of Jeffrey. I tried to look where the old man was looking but couldn't without rustling the underbrush. After he entered the building and the door closed behind him, I wiggled my raw fingers loose and took careful steps backward as I kept my eyes on the door.

I found the railroad tracks and walked along them whispering Jeffrey's name every few feet. After a while, he whispered back my name. I was happy he was okay and regretted my fun and games.

We got away this time. There would not be another. •

Never Underestimate an Old Man

Carlton Clayton lives in Charlotte, North Carolina, where he is a volunteer with the North Carolina Writer's Network Prison Outreach Program and a member of the Charlotte Writer's Club. He got his real start in writing at Charlotte Center for Literary Arts where he wrote the story that appears here. He is at work on a memoir about growing up along the Neuse River aptly titled "Along the Banks of the Neuse." Carlton also has work in *Pembroke Magazine* and the *New York Quarterly.*

In the Form of a Child

by Sarah H. Clarke

Madie had to choose between her mother and her father. She'd been lugging her stuff back and forth between them weekly ever since she could remember. The older she got, the more stuff she had to lug. At 15, she was just tired of moving.

She'd agonized over the decision for a long time, not wanting to hurt either parent. Her mom, Sarah, was younger, had a long-term career, a steady relationship with a nice guy and provided Madie a stable, conventional upbringing. Her dad, Harry, on the other hand, was much older, frequently out of work, struggled with finances, and never could maintain a romantic relationship. His parenting was erratic, distracted. A lifelong artist, he spent his time painting giant landscapes, donning the same jeans and paint-smeared t-shirt for days and ignoring an ever-expanding gray afro. Between his nicotine-stained fingers continually burned a hand-rolled Bali Shag cigarette.

When Madie was an infant, doctors performed an emergency procedure on Harry to insert a stent into his coronary artery.

But the ongoing cholesterol medicine didn't agree with him, so he quit taking it. He continued smoking, insisting the Surgeon General's warning was a conspiracy and screaming "government overreach" in response to smoking bans. He continued to eat whatever he wanted, rebuffing anyone who tried to tell him otherwise. He was a staunch believer in rugged individualism and autonomy. No one, not any doctor, and certainly not the government, was going to tell him what to do with his own body.

Even at a young age, Madie had ideas about where her dad should improve. She encouraged him to wear clean t-shirts, cut his toenails, quit smoking. Harry wasn't easy to corral, and his temper flared at the slightest of perceived criticisms. But she knew how to maneuver him and, as a teenager, that included countering his angry rants with ones of her own. If he would listen to anyone, it would be her—and they both knew it. With her prodding, he did improve his daily existence when she was with him: cooked real food instead of frozen dinners, restricted his smoking to one room, kept a regular sleep schedule, engaged in outdoor activities. They grew carrots in clay pots, hiked and biked through the neighborhood, and went swimming in the community pool. They made artwork together, photography, and music. Madie knew her dad needed her, and it was that understanding that made up her mind. She would tell her parents that she wanted to live full time with him.

Sarah took the news on the phone with empathy. She'd always said the custody arrangement could be changed to meet Madie's growing needs. When Madie told her dad in person, he was taken by complete surprise. The house boomed with his bellowing voice—something about not being consulted, all the responsibility being dumped on him, and child support. But as usual, his temper was short-lived and within an hour he'd reverted back to his amiable side, imagining life with his daughter all to himself. The monotony of coming up with dinner ... every ... single ... night, making sure she did her homework, getting her to and from school, and all the in-between made him want to run very far away. But, of course, he would do it—for her.

It was late that same October afternoon when Madie found her dad lying on the sidewalk, his face submerged in an empty flowerpot. Agonizing dread seized her, followed by a throng of uniforms, onlooking neighbors, flashing lights. The rever-berating anxiety of those two hours surged with the deafening words of a downcast officer. Harry was gone.

Sometimes it's hard to make sense of this life, why Madie's brave, hard-made choice was so cruelly reversed. Sarah kept a close eye on her daughter for months following the tragedy, awaiting an emotional fallout that never came.

That spring, they went on a cross-country road trip to the Grand Canyon. Madie needed driving hours for her license and they both needed a vacation. The trip rendered life-long memories and a chance to continue to heal as the Great Plains blurred past them along old Route 66.

Over the following year, Madie got her first job, finished her sophomore classes, and got her driver's license, which she kept in a wallet that was once her father's. Sarah began to let go of her hypervigilance, and life moved on.

While Harry's sudden death was sooner than his loved ones wanted, he no doubt lived a longer, happier life than he otherwise would have, because of Madie. It's often thought that guardian angels covertly love and protect us from beyond the veil. Perhaps, in certain hard-headed cases, an angel is deployed directly on the ground in the form most likely to change a person's life—that of a child. •

Sarah H. Clarke lives in Charlotte, North Carolina, and has privately written non-fiction since her teens. She recently joined the Charlotte Writers Club and looks forward to forging new relationships with fellow writers. Married with two children and five stepchildren, she and her husband live in an 18th century home that they all restored together. International travel and the study of social sciences and metaphysical topics are among her passions, as well as maintaining a strong connection with our natural environment and inducing the creative flow in all she does.

Stranded

by Karen Luke Jackson

The steering wheel shakes as I crest a hill on I-240 in Asheville, North Carolina, headed for the University of North Carolina at Asheville library to complete a research paper. I pull the sedan onto the shoulder, turn my flashers on, and exit to see what's wrong. Just as I suspect: left rear tire flat.

Owning no CB radio and with mobile phones a distant dream, I slide back into the driver's seat and wait for another motorist to stop. Cars whiz by, seemingly taking no notice. An hour later, I begin to fret. My husband doesn't expect me home until 8 o'clock. Soon it will be too dark to hike several miles to the next exit where I know there's a gas station. *I can't just sit here!*

I open the glove compartment, rummage for the car's manual, and slide my index finger down its table of contents scanning for how to change a tire. *Why didn't I take that powder puff mechanics class the community college offered?* I read the instructions, get back out of the car, holding the guide in my hand, and open the trunk. *Where's the spare, the jack?*

I fail to notice a red compact that parks behind me until a large-boned African American woman, gray hair framing her face, asks, "Honey, are you okay?"

"Yes, and thanks so much for stopping. Do you know how to change a tire?"

"Sure don't, but I'm not leaving 'til you're safe."

Naomi tells me she was on her way to a Sunday night Bible study in Asheville when she spotted me on the side of the road. I'm concerned she'll be late. "Taking care of you is more important," she says.

Knowing I'll want to thank this Good Samaritan when the ordeal is over, I scribble her name, address, and phone number in a notebook. We're discussing the option of her driving me to the gas station so I can call home when a pick-up with an ear-splitting muffler pulls behind her car. Two men in their twenties wearing baseball caps hop out. Brothers, they tell us.

"Do you ladies need any help changing that tire?"

"Do we!" we say.

"We would've been here sooner but we were headed to Canton when we saw your predicament. Had to drive to the next exit and circle back."

Surrounded by these three rescuers, I don't know whether to laugh or cry. Twenty minutes later, the younger man throws the tattered wheel and the jack into the trunk and slams the lid.

"Can I get your names and addresses?" I ask the guys. "I'd like to pay you for your time or send a gift to show my thanks."

"No worries, ma'am," these do-gooders assure me.

After they leave, I turn to Naomi. "I'm so sorry you missed your meeting. Until you stopped, I was petrified." We share a warmhearted embrace before she departs.

Exhausted from the afternoon's events, I abandon plans to visit the library and return home. My husband, distracted by bath-time for our two children, doesn't even notice that I'm disheveled and late. When we're in bed, I share what happened.

"I could have been stuck there all night, even mugged! Would you have noticed if I hadn't come home?"

"But you're here now and okay," he reminds me as he plumps his pillow and turns off the light.

The next morning, I ignore his protests over the high price tag of a bag phone and purchase one for my car. I also call a gift shop in Waynesville and order a floral arrangement to be delivered to Naomi.

That afternoon, the florist calls. The address I gave her does not exist. The phone number is no longer in service. *Did I transpose the numbers? Write the information down wrong?*

Stranded

67

For a week, I call different combinations of the phone number, search property and tax records. Not a clue turns up. *Did she give me a fake phone number? A false address?*

I stop searching when it dawns on me that there's another possibility: that my mother's stories about guardian angels are true. She avowed that one time at the ocean when she was too far out, an angel guided her safely to shore. And so, like her, I want to believe that Heaven dispatched three unlikely protectors, disguised as people, to aid me that night, to calm my fears, to lend a helping hand right there on Interstate 240. But even more, I want to believe in goodness: that people can be angels, appearing when we are stranded, seeking nothing in return, and leaving us to wonder at the miracle of it all. •

Karen Luke Jackson (Flat Rock, North Carolina) draws upon oral history, contemplative practices and nature for inspiration. Her work has appeared in *Nobody's Home, moonShine review,* and *Emrys Journal;* two poetry collections, *The View Ever Changing* and *GRIT;* and *The Story Mandala: Finding Wholeness in a Divided World.* A member of the North Carolina Writers' Network and the North Carolina Poetry Society, Karen resides in a cottage on a goat pasture. There she writes and companions people on their spiritual journeys.

In Waves

by Elaine Thomas

I turned to see David bouncing in the waves, arms flailing, yelling for help. Instinctively I moved toward him. As much as I might like to look back and think I got into trouble heroically trying to save my cousin, the more probable truth is that we were caught in a rip current, a hazard frequently encountered along the Carolina coast. Within seconds both of us were struggling to keep our heads above water, gasping for air and trying not to swallow the sea.

No lifeguard was on duty. We desperately yelled for David's parents who had turned their eyes away from us just long enough to speak to another nice couple. They wore street clothes. They had come onto the beach only to indulge David's and my insistent pleas to swim one last time before the drive home.

I could feel myself being pulled into deeper and deeper water, too weak to fight so powerful a force. In a sense the sea is mother to us all. We carry her in our bodies, feel her rhythms and tides in the pumping of our own hearts. In our natural love for Mother Ocean, it can become easy to drown in her vast, fluid embrace.

David's father looked our way, checking on us. I had never seen the man move so fast. As he tore across the sand in our direction, he unbuttoned and threw aside his shirt. A former Marine, he knew clothes would weigh him down when he hit the water. He unbuckled and kicked off his pants. I was a kid, a little girl; even in the midst of drowning, my thought was a stunned, *Uncle Bill is in his underwear.*

He reached me and moved past, trying to save his son. I felt his strong hand hit the center of my back and shove me forward toward shallower water. As another wave broke over my head, I feared his push would not be enough.

Then my aunt, my mother's youngest sister, who I had not seen run fully clothed behind her husband into the water, grabbed my arm and pulled me toward her, dragging me out of danger. She kept a tight grasp on me until we reached firm footing. We stood shivering and watched as Bill brought his son, held tightly against his bare chest, to join us there, safely on shore.

Guilt and relief rode with us all the way home. I vaguely remember stopping for ice cream and an intense discussion of whether my grandmother, with whom I lived, needed to hear the full story. (She clearly did not.) I also remember an unstated, uncomfortable half-thought in the back of my own head, a thought I doubt anyone else entertained: *What if only one of us could have been saved?*

Like I said, uncomfortable—for me.

After I recovered, at least for the most part, from my wave of anxiety over Bill stepping past me to save his son, I recognized with gratitude that my uncle and aunt had indeed prevented me from drowning. They rescued me because they loved me (and because they wisely feared my grandmother), but I feel confident they would have tried to save me even if I were some never-before-seen stranger's child. We come into the world alone, and as the specific child of someone, but we move through it as the single wave moves on the sea, part of the whole.

Many years after that troublesome day Mother Ocean drew me home again, this time for good. I live near those same waters. I walk along that beach. I have changed a great deal through the years. The sea, the sky, the sands shift and change every day.

Old, young, and in-between, people in all stages of life roll by. As I walk, I admire the oncoming generations. Dozens of training lifeguards pass me, running. They are beautiful, every one of them. In years past I might have been tempted to fake another near-drowning by way of introduction. Now I find myself happy just to see so much unleashed energy and promise. They radiate self-confidence. With them in charge, everything before us feels brighter, somehow trouble-free. Another generational wave, the smallest children are sheer joy to watch. They escape their parents and splash squealing into the water, mothers and fathers in pursuit. For children the age I was on that long-ago day, a local "surf school" looks to be

In Waves

at full enrollment. One by one, young surfers rise to their feet, standing proudly on short boards as they ride a wave to shore. Adults watching them cheer and applaud for every child, whether their own or the child of strangers. They all applaud our future. •

Elaine Thomas lives in Wilmington, North Carolina, and is a member of the Wilmington Write to Publish group. Her work has appeared in numerous literary journals and magazines, including *The Dead Mule School of Southern Literature, moonShine Review, Blue Mountain Review,* and *Pembroke Magazine.* She won the North Carolina Writers' Network 2018 Rose Post Creative Nonfiction Competition. A retired college communications professional, Thomas also holds an M.Div. from Duke Divinity School and now works with New Hanover Regional Medical Center as an on-call hospital chaplain.

Let It Go

by Suzanne Cottrell

My husband had Memorial Day off, but I had to teach, making up for a snow day. I drank a whole bottle of water on my drive home, so as soon as I entered our house, I set down my bag and dashed to the bathroom. From the toilet, my peripheral vision caught a dark blob. I leaned toward the tub and saw what looked like a piece of black hose. *Why is a hose in the bathtub?* My pulse quickened after considering the possibilities.

I yelled to my husband who was grilling cheeseburgers on the front porch, "Bob, did you put a rubber snake in the bathtub? Not funny."

"If there's a snake in the bathtub, it's real."

My pupils widened; I gasped and hiked up my pants as I sprinted to my husband. "How did a snake get there?"

"What did it look like?"
"Black and slick."
"Sounds like a black rat snake slithered through a crack."

I cringed as I imagined a rat crawling through too. I tugged my husband's shirt. "You need to come look, now!"

"I'm starving, and the burgers are ready. I'll handle it
after dinner."
"But what if it gets out? We might not find it."
"It's in the bathtub. It's not going anywhere."

My stomach churned. "You'd better be right. I don't want
to see it slithering across the kitchen floor while I'm eating."

I bit into my cheeseburger and glanced at the floor. Even
though I saw nothing, I pulled my legs under me and kept
scanning the floor. *What if I had decided to take a shower?*
I shuddered. "How can we remove it?"

"I'm not sure."

As soon as we finished eating, we headed to the bathroom.
He examined the snake as it struggled to maneuver the
smooth, sloped porcelain. Unable to get traction, it slid to the
bottom. We noted the identifying white throat and chin.

With raised eyebrows, I stared at my husband. "You're not
going to pick it up, are you?"

"No. It's not poisonous, but it can bite." The 4-foot snake
vibrated its tail and flicked its tongue. "Get a garbage bag
and the broom. I'll see if I can sweep it into the bag."

I grabbed my husband's arm. "Wait. You're not expecting me
to hold the bag."
"Just get the broom and bag."

After I scurried to retrieve the items, my husband grabbed

the broom. "Hold the bag open. When I get the snake inside, clamp the bag shut. Don't worry."

Rubbing the back of my neck, *I can do this.* I leaned over the side of the tub and held the bag. I wanted to close my eyes, but I didn't dare. My husband nudged the snake. As the broom bristles brushed against the snake, it raised its head, opened its mouth, hissed, and struck at the bag. I screamed, dropped the plastic bag, and jumped back.

"Are you okay?"
"No, that snake almost bit my hand." I gripped the door frame with sweaty palms. My heart raced. "Just give me a minute."

My husband swept up the bag and handed it to me. I asked, "Why don't you hold the bag, and I'll sweep the snake into it?"

He shook the bag at me. "Just hold it."

I squinted, leaned over the tub, and held the bag. My hands trembled. "Hurry, hurry!"

With one stroke, my husband swept the snake into the bag, dropped the broom, and snatched the closed bag from me. He twisted it and carried the bag away from his body as he left the house and walked toward the woods.

"What will you do with it?" I shouted after him.
"Let it go."
"What if it comes back?" I crossed my arms and clutched my sides. My eyes remained glued to the garbage bag. My husband shrugged his shoulders.

As he approached the woods, two women labored up the hill

Let It Go

on their daily walk.

"Good evening ladies, lovely weather."
The taller woman asked, "Whatcha got in that bag?"
"A black snake."
"A what!" said the other woman, staring at the bag with a
gaping mouth. "What are you going to do with it?"
"Let it go."

The women's arms powered like chugging locomotives as they
climbed the hill's crest and disappeared. My husband set the
bag on the ground and jiggled it. "Okay, you're free to go,"
he said to the snake before it vanished among the leaves.

More frightened than I, the snake had left a foul-smelling musk
in the bathtub. That evening I scrubbed with disinfectant until
my muscles burned.

For weeks, I tensed every time I pulled back the shower
curtain. I was embarrassed to be so scared. My husband said to
let it go. That's why I gloated more than you can imagine when
I caught him checking the tub too—the snake. •

Suzanne Cottrell, a member of Creative Voices, Taste Life Twice
Writers, and NC Writers' Network, lives with her husband in
Granville County, NC. An outdoor enthusiast and retired teacher,
she enjoys reading, writing, knitting, hiking, and Pilates. Her prose
has appeared in numerous journals and anthologies, including the
Personal Story Publishing Project, Inwood Indiana Press, *Quail Bell
Magazine, Parks and Points,* and *Nailpolish Stories.* She's the author of
three poetry chapbooks: *Gifts of the Seasons, Autumn and Winter* ;
Gifts of the Seasons, Spring and Summer ; and *Scarred Resilience.*

Four Angry Men
by Joel Nelson

My "worry" meter was pegged: there were four angry men, each pointing a pistol at me. It was nearly midnight, and I was alone in my car, stopped on a road in a foreign country. The quartet was obviously enraged with me, but I had no idea why. I really thought my life was about to end in a fusillade of hot lead!

It had all begun so benignly. Two years earlier, I'd graduated college with an engineering degree and an ROTC commission; the latter brought with it a two-year, active-duty commitment as an Army second lieutenant. I was thrilled at being ordered to go overseas to Germany, and I proceeded to brush up on my two years of high-school German.

However, once I arrived in Germany, I was rudely greeted with another set of orders: these directed me to France! "FRANCE??" I loudly protested, to no avail. The phrase "Needs of The Service" rang in my ears as I grudgingly rode the train from Frankfurt, Germany, to Paris, France. All I knew about France was that the Eiffel Tower was there, and they ate snails.

My duty station was in the town of Saran, a northern suburb of the city of Orleans. Orleans is located about an hour's drive south of Paris. The duty was pleasant enough and I soon adapted to my new surroundings. I had never owned a new car and quickly rectified that situation with the purchase of a new 1960 MG. By today's standards, the MG's 78 horsepower was just this side of "feeble," but I fancied myself a hotshot driver of my new sports car. On a long enough stretch of road, it would just touch 100 mph.

At that time, one of my unspoken ambitions was to someday qualify for the Indy 500, America's foremost racing event in Indianapolis, Indiana. I held no hopes of winning that world-famous event but thought I might eventually develop enough expertise to be among the 33 starters. To that end, I availed myself of any opportunity to hone my driving skills.
I attended a couple of European race-driving schools and did well at each of them. In addition, I ran amateur competition events whenever my free time and $2500/year salary would allow.

I would sometimes leave the vinyl competition numbers affixed to the flanks of the MG for days after these events, as I thought that doing so gave me a certain flair on the local highways. I considered myself a safe driver on those roads, and always obeyed traffic lights and stop signs. But speed limits? Well, maybe not so much. On major French highways, there were no speed limits, but on secondary roads there certainly were.

The French were initially thrilled to see the Americans arrive on their shores on 6 June 1944, but by the time I arrived 16 years later, not all Frenchmen were quite so delighted. In all fairness, had I been in their shoes, I might've felt the same: several thousand young American GIs living in your towns, drinking your wine, and wooing your *madamoiselles* might've contributed to occasional friction in Franco-American relations.

My army-issued BOQ (Bachelor Officers' Quarters) were in Olivet, on the south side of Orleans, and my workplace in Saran was about 10 miles away, on the north side of Orleans. On this particular evening I was to report to work at midnight and had timed my journey so I'd arrive 10 or 15 minutes early. At that hour, Orleans traffic was nonexistent, so I didn't exactly dawdle en route. In retrospect, I youthfully rationalized that running 20-30 kilometers per hour over the speed limit didn't really apply to me: I was a budding race driver. Besides, going fast was FUN!

As I approached my Saran destination, there was a stop sign and, as always, I obeyed it. As I halted, a wheezy old Peugeot sedan came steaming up behind me, and four *gendarmes* burst forth, their guns drawn. They knew I was a GI before they stopped me, as our license plates were different from those used by French civilians. And I imagine my racing numbers, still on the car, may have contributed to their attitude. Turns out that, unbeknownst to me, they'd been chasing me for three or four miles, unable to catch me until the stop sign.

Once they saw that I was cooperative, sober, and neatly dressed in my khaki uniform, they holstered their artillery and began interrogating me. Through my minimal French and their fractured English, their concern about my *vitesse* (speed) emerged. I quickly found myself apologizing for every "Ugly American" whose presence had sullied *la belle France* since D-Day. (And I admit some groveling might have been involved.)

Eventually they let me go after a stern chewing-out. I monitored my in-town speed more closely thereafter.

I never qualified for Indy. •

Joel Nelson lives in Marietta, Georgia. As a 4th-grade schoolboy in 1946, he wrote a two-paragraph essay on the meaning of freedom; a half-dozen of those words ended up being quoted in The Boston Globe. This is his first published work since. After 20 years in the U.S. Army followed by 30 as a physician assistant working in a psychiatric hospital, he's been retired since 2009.

In Bear Country

by Barbara Houston

"**I**t's a bear! RUN!"

The frightened couple shouted as they flew past us down the narrow, winding, mountain path. My husband, Jerry, and I looked up and spotted a large black bear about 50 feet away running toward us. Immobilized by fear, we stood for seconds unsure what to do. Our first instinct was to run for our lives and follow the other couple down the trail.

"Wait," I said to Jerry, remembering the ranger talk we had attended. "Do **not** run from a bear," the ranger said. "Make yourselves as small as you can and cover your heads, so you don't look threatening."

Frantic, we looked for someplace to hide. There was nowhere we could escape the approaching danger, so we stepped off the footpath into the scrubby underbrush which provided minimal cover. I dropped to my knees, crouched down with my face in the dirt, clasped both hands behind my neck, and prayed that the bear would pass us by. Bending down on one knee in front of me, Jerry lowered his head but kept his eyes on the approaching animal. "I'm watching him," he said. "He's still running down the path."

Terrified and vulnerable, I visualized a slow, excruciating death with giant 6-inch claws ripping through my back like knives cutting through soft butter. Would the bear eat my flesh or simply toss me around like a dog playing with a toy? How long would it take to die? I knew that Jerry would defend me. Would the monster attack him first while I listened helplessly to his screams? Both scenarios were too horrible to imagine.

"He's still on the path," my protector-husband whispered while gently patting my back. Terrorized by approaching doom, we awaited our fate. "He stopped running. He sees us," Jerry said, "and he looks confused." We remained quiet and unmoving. The horror of the unknown continued for what seemed an eternity, until Jerry spoke again in a surprised voice, "Wait! The bear went off the trail. He's going around us. Now he's getting back onto the trail below and is continuing on the path down the hill. He's avoiding us!"

We stayed in that spot for several minutes to give the bear time to get as far away as possible. It took all the courage we could muster to walk down the path, but we had no other way out.

The ranger had said, "You are in bear country. You are invading their living room, so ring the doorbell and let them know you're there. Make a lot of loud noise because they want to avoid you, too." We headed down the footpath for several seemingly interminable minutes. We sang and yelled as loudly as we could. We were scared and anxious knowing we remained in grave danger. *Was the bear nearby? Would he attack us? Were there other bears around?* Not knowing was intimidating!

What a relief we felt when we entered a clearing next to the lower falls! We saw the couple who had run past us talking with several other hikers. Because we had not followed them, they thought we might have been attacked. We were grateful they too had made it safely to that point. Several of the group were looking expectantly up the trail; when they spotted us coming around the bend, they began shouting, cheering, and clapping. After explaining to everyone what had happened, Jerry and I headed toward the trail entrance. Two rangers with rifles headed toward us. They had been warned of our danger.

Although extremely nervous from this episode, we continued to hike in "bear country," but we took several precautions. Aware of our surroundings, we made a lot of noise on those hikes—singing and shouting at the top of our lungs. We bought an expensive can of bear spray. It was supposed to stun a bear from several feet away, giving us enough time to escape. *But would we be able to use it if we actually spotted another bear?* Thankfully, we never had to find out. That was our only encounter with a bear.

What had begun that day as a leisurely hike to the upper falls at Glacier National Park in Montana could have ended in disaster. If we had run behind the other couple, we may have been chased by the bear, and we could have been maimed or killed.

In Bear Country

Because we did the right things, our life-and-death adventure had a positive outcome. We escaped the Montana black bear and lived to tell about it. •

Barbara Houston lives in Charlotte, North Carolina. A member of an informal writing group, the Scribblers, she is currently writing her memoirs. After college, Barbara taught English for four years. Later, she served as Director of Human Resources at Discovery Place Museum in Charlotte for over ten years. Now retired, Barbara enjoys her writing project, reading fiction, singing, spending time with family and friends, and traveling with her husband, Jerry.

Family Troubles
by Bill Donohue

My father developed polio as a young boy and died after a 5-year battle with ALS. My son was born with Down syndrome and Muscular Dystrophy (MD).

Trouble comes packaged differently to every family. We've had our share. Medical packages tend to be a role of the dice. It doesn't matter how they arrive, you just deal. We learn different ways to care and to give care.

There is a nuanced difference. I learned about caring from my mother, homemaker and Sunday school teacher. I learned about caregiving from my wife, the nurse practitioner.

When I was 3, I lined up dimes atop 2x4s on cement blocks lining Main Street. My mom said, "Billy, this is really important." I did not understand at the time it was part of a "March" for polio awareness. Part of not being aware of its importance to Dad was because my mother chose not to focus on Dad's disability, but rather his ability. Despite his significant limp and disfiguring hunchback, he was a state senator and civic leader.

Family Troubles

My son's FSH (Facio-Scapular-Humeral) MD was a genetic hand-me-down from his mother, the nurse who taught me caregiving. It's a far more challenging reality than his Down syndrome, but less visible, definable, or defensible. Caring for him was to expand his community access and independence against ignorant teachers, nervous employers, or mean peers. Caregiving was to help him cope with the pain of end-of-year testing, the inability to date tall blonde cheerleaders, and to see his sister leave for college while staying home, though both attended the same high school.

Caring for Dad was hard. Stubborn, proud, indomitable throughout life. Caregiving was both physical as he gained weight and lost muscle and emotional as he resisted in every way his terminal diagnosis. Bathing and feeding him as a son were especially hard for both of us.

I came to believe that caring was something nurtured over time, taught largely by example. Mom was a great example. Caregiving was often something you were thrust into. My son's explosive diarrhea emerged after a hospitalization with aspiration pneumonia. It presented in the mall, at the Y, and during his work at a restaurant. It did not offer much time for nurturing. It was an immediate, auto-pilot challenge with dignity, hygiene, and exit strategy. There was no script to share that he was now a tube-feeder, his formula and digestive system were out of sync, and that it was vital for him to be where he thrived, in the community, regaining the efferves- cence that was his character. My wife was and remains my mentor on this front.

Communication stands as the gold standard for all caregiving as I know it. Being raised in an environment that values all humanity and nature helps, as does realizing that we all are only temporarily abled. When my father lost his voice—as his grandson's now fades—the ability to express needs becomes acute. Sometimes the acuteness is simply to know you are paying attention, at other times a medical necessity. Both are part of the deal my son commands.

Communicating with my wife about caregiving, however, presents another challenge. She knew tube feeding, changing soiled linen, and communicating long before we met.
She understood as second nature more than I will ever grasp. That she carried the DNA, not of the Down syndrome but the Muscular Dystrophy, meant that she too was losing muscle: First, her abdominals, effecting posture and gait, then upper body strength impacting dressing, hair and make-up routines, and from the beginning, her ability to fully close her eyes and to smile. Moreover, she bore the reality that the young man we cherish was increasingly going to face what she had known painfully, academically, and personally nearly all his life.

Caregiving for her heart, mind, body, and spirit raises the dad, husband, and care-giving-student standard to a whole new level.

Trouble often presents double-edged circumstances which motivate and inspire. That my son, like his granddad, went on to a 4-year collegiate experience was rare. To become a 5-sport special Olympian and national para-karate champion did not arise from caring or caregiving as much as from a community of support. My wife's success launching North Carolina's first four book clubs for adults with disabilities and being named Volunteer of the Year by The Arc of North Carolina, as well, sprung from a community recognizing passion and need, a community which took her lead.

Bathing Dad was fleeting. Helping my wife and son sustain their independence is today. But the roles are reciprocal; caregivers need care as well. Love is the best antidote to most trouble. I am flush, every day with the caregiver's antidote. •

Bill Donohue is a disability advocate living in Winston Salem, North Carolina. Most of his writing (ncwaiveractionteam.com) informs and prods legislative inertia for the 15,000 with Developmental Disabilities waiting a decade or more for services while potential caregivers struggle for a living wage. Bill's first novel is a family's saga with early onset dementia, chronicled in *The Kind of September*, Amazon (2013).

Fishing Pumpkin Island

by Joe Brown

*B*OY! *Am I ever in trouble. How am I going to tell Mom and Dad I lost my little brother in the raging river when it hasn't even rained!!*

During the long, hot summer of 1968, Kirk and Clay Lawson, Bobby Grubbs, and I cooked up a plan to spend the night camping and fishing on a small rock island in the middle of the Yadkin River.

We all lived in the area of Davie County, North Carolina, called "Fork," sort of between Lexington and Mocksville on Highway 64.

As we began our 10 minutes of planning, my little brother, Carl, who was four years younger than our "experienced" average of 16, got wind of our plans and went begging Mom to let him go, too.

With Mom's blessing, we started rounding up the necessary supplies: a few old patch work quilts for bedding, a little grub, consisting of a few cans of pork and beans (no can opener), a small camp shovel (the "can opener"), and one flashlight. With only this and a handful of old Zebco fishing rods and a can of red worms, we were ready.

Our campsite was, and still is, called Pumpkin Island by the locals. (Just don't go looking for it on any map!) It rises above the normal water level all of about eight feet. It is a roundish boulder with a few cracks running around it, similar to a pumpkin. Sometimes a few small willows grow from some of the cracks, and downstream is usually a sandbar "tail," all totaling no more than two to three hundred square feet in area. The only resident of the island I ever saw was a 12-inch "skill pot" turtle, not the scientific name, but that's what we called them.

Stuffing our supplies in the old 1950 Chevy's trunk, we said our goodbyes to Mom and piled in for the short trip up River View Road, turned right onto a farm lane, and soon arrived at the Sugar Shack.

The shack was a rough pole structure with a tin roof and 2-foot-wide shelves on three sides like tables to eat off. This picnic shelter was the location for many fish fry's and a good place for fishermen to gather and lie about the fish they had caught. The shack was upstream about 100 yards from Pumpkin Island.

Before we departed on our Island adventure, I made a beeline for Bony Hendrix's watermelon patch. The cannonball watermelons grown in the Yadkin river bottoms are the best! *And, shucks, he wouldn't miss just one.*

We slipped down the dirt bank of the river with supplies firmly in grasp and into the rushing current. The water felt good. The river splits to go around the island. On the far side was a deep rapid; on our side, the water was only 12 to 16 inches deep, but it moved fast over smooth, slick river rocks. Upstream from the island, many scattered boulders stuck up from the water.

It was slow going but we eased over to the sand bar behind the main rock. We were all in high spirits and commenced to enjoy the fishing and just hanging out. The fish just would not cooperate, but we did catch a couple. Since we didn't have a gas lantern to fish with, after nightfall we decided to hit the quilts when it finally got dark. We were pretty tired from all the day's activities anyhow. I know I was out like a light.

Sometime after midnight . . . Boooomm . . . Boooomm.
We all sat up.

"What was that!!" we all asked at the same time. BOOOOMM!

"Who's got the light??"

"Clay's got it. It sounds like it's coming from upriver."

"Sweep it up that way."

That's when we saw a 55-gallon drum coming downstream and banging on the boulders.

"That's weird!"

Fishing Pumpkin Island

"Look the river is really close!" Shinning the light around the island, it didn't take long to realize the river had risen well over a foot. The sandbar was gone.

A thunderstorm upriver was making the water rise downstream. With a mad rush we gathered everything we could find in the dark and abandoned our island. Forming a human chain, we started easing across the flooding water. We leaned into the almost waist-deep current, just barely moving our feet to keep any footing at all.

How am I going to tell Mom that I lost Carl to the raging river?

Somehow, with the Lord's help, after what seemed ages, we made it to the bank and stumbled back to the Sugar Shack, where we took advantage of the shelves to sleep the rest of the night.

As I drifted off to sleep, I thought, *Thank you Lord! Now I don't have to face Mama about losing my little brother.* •

Joseph Brown is a native of North Carolina, born in Yadkin County and reared in Davie County. He now resides in the Bethania area of Forsyth County and has lived all his life within 40 miles of his birthplace. In February 2020 he retired from 50 years in the construction industry. Most of his previous writing has been daily journals on his mission trips to Kentucky, Canada, and Ecuador. His earlier published stories appeared in 2019, 2020, and spring 2021 Personal Story Publishing Projects.

Trouble Came with the Moonshine

by Phyliss Grady Adcock

My mother's childhood reads like an unbelievable novel set in rural eastern North Carolina. Life in her dysfunctional home, run by or ruined by an alcoholic father, took twists and turns that few could ever imagine or even want to.

The four children were like stair steps, two to three years apart. My mother was the oldest and remembered the most of their shared childhoods, stories she passed on to me because I liked to write about her upbringing.

My maternal grandfather was an exceptional athlete, a card shark, and a billiards player. People were drawn to him because of his magnetic personality, and they excused his shortcomings such as his lack of self-control. That circumstance got him offered a job running the local pool hall. This was a great fit for his family because upstairs included a kitchen, a crude bath, and enough bedrooms for his brood. Housing had been a problem because my grandfather could not hold on to rent money long enough to meet his monthly obligations. Now, at least, his family could count on a place to sleep, as his "magnetic personality" packed the poolroom every night.

That pool hall was the local hangout. After supper and on weekends, men went there to escape home and to tell tales and swap lies. It had a grill, chairs for playing checkers and poker, lots of tables for billiards, and spittoons. The walls displayed the latest risqué calendars, sent to all pool halls back then. The favorites remained up even as the passing years made them useless, like some of the patrons. And moonshine was served from the broom closet, placed there because it was illegal—Prohibition. The moonshine was poured into Mason jars and arranged on shelves for quick dispensing. My grandfather could vouch for how good it tasted because he was also in charge of "quality control" on a daily basis.

Each night after everyone had left, he would tidy up. He'd scrape the greasy grill, carry out the trash, and empty the spittoons. His last job of the night was to pour moonshine into those filthy, smelly spittoons. He declared that if moonshine could purge all the sin out of Hell, it could certainly clean those spittoons.

Late one night, one of the local deputies who loved the moonshine, overheard that the pool hall would be raided. He tipped off my grandfather; the deputy did not want to lose his source of moonshine. And my grandfather did not want to get caught with it. That's when he woke up his family so four sleepy children and my grandmother could help pour the suspect spirits down the upstairs drain. They formed an assembly line to make the process more efficient. By the time the Sheriff arrived nothing remained but spotless, empty jars arranged on shelves and four confused little children.

But where you have willing customers and suppliers, commerce will not be denied. Within 24 hours the containers were refilled, the closet restocked, and everything was again ready for business. Men rolled into the pool hall and another night of Southern mischief began. After cleaning up, my grandfather went upstairs and got ready for bed, but he had forgotten to lock the downstairs door. One of the patrons who had left his hat returned to retrieve it. On the way out, the fellow threw his lighted cigar butt into one of the spittoons—one just recently cleaned with moonshine.

The smoldering cigar and the alcohol fumes soon became friends and began to sizzle. The heat soon rose and high-octane jars on the shelves began to explode. The whole family awoke to a storm of breaking jars and tiny fires spreading throughout the broom closet. Once again, my grandmother and her four sleepy children came to the rescue. They formed a "bucket brigade" and doused the inferno completely using pots and pans full of water.

By the time the local fire truck arrived—summoned by neighbors to project their adjacent homes—only charred walls and broken glass remained. Amidst the smell of alcohol permeating the night air, stood four pitiful children in bedclothes, wiping their sooty faces. No one asked any questions. No one offered any help.

Trouble Came with the Moonshine

As was his practice, my grandfather gave no words of thanks to his small army, which always jumped when they heard him sound revelry. This would not be the last of the trouble this family of troopers would face. Their childhoods produced four strong adults who could weather storms, solve problems, roll with life's punches, smile through tears, show great compassion for the underdogs of life, and still find humor in really strange situations! If it is true that trouble that does not kill us makes us stronger, these four should by now be nearly invincible. •

After teaching for 34 years, Phyliss Grady Adcock, retired in Morehead City, North Carolina. Her writing has appeared in *Mailbox Magazine, Teacher's Helper, That Southern Thing* and *Luck and Opportunity*. Her grant writing netted over $5,000 for classroom projects. For one grant proposal, she was recognized as the first Raychem Educator of the Year. She is listed in Who's Who Among America's Teachers for 1996 and 2000. She is currently writing humorous stories about the colorful characters in her family. Writing is her "Happy Place."

Resilience

by Regina Lobree

"Resilience." The word caught hold of me as I read the editorial page in The Winston-Salem Journal. And then the famous picture of Jesse Owens in a running stance at the 1936 Olympics brought a smile to my face as I gazed over to the framed photo of my dad with Jesse Owens, one taken in California in 1975. The two men had never met until then, although both, a Black and a Jew, were in Berlin in 1936, one to participate in the Olympic games, the other to coach a women's track and field team from Austria.

My dad grew up in Vienna. He wanted to do something in sports; track and field was the cheapest thing to do, so he ran. High schools had no sports, so at 16 he joined the Vienna Athletic Club. He kept this secret from his parents! Once in college, he had to remain part of the club team; being Jewish, he was unable to participate on a school team. He continued his running career after college, and by 1931, at age 22, he set a record in the Austrian Championship, running the 100-meter event in 11 seconds. He was also part of the 4x100 relay team and the medley relay team, each setting Austrian records.

In 1932, Dad and six other athletes were honored as the country's top track and field athletes. He was also inaugurated into the Austrian Athletic Federation. And all that led to his being at the 1936 Olympics. Because of his outstanding career in sport, he was asked to be part of—and to head up— Austria's delegation of 37 relay torch runners carrying the Olympic flame across Austria toward Berlin.

Controversy swirled among his sport colleagues about his wanting to participate in games being held in a country where Jews were being persecuted. He was not looked upon favorably by the Jewish athletic club in Vienna. But for Dad, sport was more than religion. Jews were not allowed to compete in Nazi Germany, but they were allowed access to the Olympic Games. My dad ran with the torch, at night, one kilometer, the last leg through Austria to the Czech border, ever fearful the flame might go out. The morning after his run, Dad boarded a train bound for Berlin to watch the Olympic flame enter the stadium. A few days later, as sports director of the Austrian women's track and field team, he marched past where Hitler and his staff were seated. Although the Olympics in Berlin were devoid of open antisemitism and were not overshadowed by German propaganda, it all changed when Jesse Owens competed and won his four gold medals. Jesse Owens defied Hitler's Aryan supremacy ideology, and my dad marveled at Owen's accomplishment and admired him greatly. It was my dad's wish to meet Jesse Owens personally and to shake his hand, which he got to do 40 years later. Both men survived the discrimination and persecution each encountered to tell their stories.

After the Berlin Olympics, my father returned to Vienna. At the time of the Nazi invasion in March 1938, Dad was in graduate school and was the athletic trainer for the Baron and Baroness Rothschild. Soon after, he sought and secured sponsorship to come to America, but his passage to America did not happen before *Kristallnacht*, November 9, 1938. His escape was harrowing as he hid on a rooftop one evening, to avoid being "rounded up" on the way to his college classes.

Dad left Vienna on November 28, bound for New York. His sponsors secured an apartment and a job for him but would not help him with securing passage for his parents. By the time he was able to sponsor them on his own, the American consulate had closed. His parents were deported in 1941 and perished in 1942 in the Treblinka Extermination Camp.

My father died in 2002 at the age of 92. He lived a good life despite the troubles he encountered. He married, raised a family, and was proud to be a Jew, despite what he had faced. He and my mother raised me to be a proud Jew as well, despite the antisemitism in this country. Having raised two children and being a grandmother, if I could today, I would ask my father so much more: his feelings the day he left his parents; did he think he would see them again; did he have survivor's guilt; would he have done anything differently?

What I do know, is that my father was a trustworthy and honest individual, a good friend, a loving husband, and a wonderful father. We all face troubles in life. Dad overcame his with resilience and thus was a blessing to our family. •

Regina Lobree lives in Clemmons, North Carolina. This is her first
written piece she has submitted for publication. Her 43-year teaching
career allowed her to share her love of reading and writing
with her students. Currently, she enjoys retirement, her grandchildren, and substitute teaching for the local school system.

Mom and Pops

by Beth Bixby Davis

My friend Leila Jane lives in Maine and helps look after her aging parents. About three years ago, Leila spent the weekend with her mom to give Mom's caretaker a break. Mom and Pops hadn't lived together for 20 years but had a civil relationship. Pops called and asked permission to come visit for the weekend, so Leila told him they would look forward to his visit. No way did she imagine the trouble this family weekend would produce.

Leila Jane put them in the bedroom with twin beds thinking that would be fine. Pops was 92 and Mom was 87. In the small cottage that night, Leila heard beds squeaking and lots of chatter and giggling coming from that room. She covered her ears and thought, *OMG, what is going on in there?*

Later in the night Leila heard Mom calling her, "Leila Jane, hurry, something's wrong with Pops." Hurrying to the room, she found Pops slurring his speech and staggering around the room. Mom also seemed to be acting a little strangely. Leila quickly called her cousin Pam, a nurse who lived close-by. Pam checked Pop's vitals which were okay, but they both thought he might be having a stroke. Not wanting to wait for an ambulance, Leila quickly got her parents in the car and drove them to the hospital.

The staff in the emergency room took Pops right in and Leila settled Mom in the waiting room, making her promise not to move. While Pops was being evaluated, Leila worked on the necessary paperwork. Returning to the waiting room she could not find Mom. Asking if anyone had seen a little lady with a floppy hat and Birkenstocks, she was pointed towards the ER. It seems Mom had told them she thought she was having a heart attack.

Just then, Leila's phone rang. The caregiver was calling. It seems while driving by and seeing all the lights on she became concerned and stopped by. Running into the house, she found Cousin Pam sprawled on the couch moaning and trying to talk with unintelligible sounds coming out of her mouth. Leila thought, *What is going on? Do we have a gas leak or something?* The caregiver had called the ambulance for Cousin Pam, fearing that she might be having a stroke. The EMTs had in turn called the fire department, who came on site running CO_2 tests on the house. In the meantime, Aunt Carol, who lived just down the street saw all the commotion and hurried to the house. The ambulance was ready to leave with Cousin Pam, so Aunt Carol followed it to the hospital.

Eventually Pops, whose condition was grim, was admitted to the Intensive Care Unit. Mom was determined to be fine— diagnosed with vertigo and dehydration—and was discharged. Leila asked Aunt Carol to please take Mom home and to stay with her; she would stay at the hospital to deal with Pops and Pam.

In a few minutes, the caregiver called Leila back to get a report. In the course of the conversation, the caretaker asked Leila what she had done with her cookies. Lelia replied that she found "those old things" on the top shelf and they were "hard as a rock." She had planned to throw them out, she said, but had forgotten and left them on the counter. With a shaky voice the caretaker said, "Leila, those were my medical marijuana prescription cookies. There were six, and there's only one left."

Leila jumped up from her seat and ran down the hall looking for the doctor. "I know what's wrong with Pops." Quietly entering the ICU, Leila and the doctor questioned Pops. He replied with slurred speech that he had eaten three cookies. "They tasted terrible, but I was so hungry."

Leila's Cousin Pam was still in the ER so the next stop was to ask her. She said, "Yes, I ate one cookie. It tasted terrible, but I was so hungry." The nurse asked with a smile, "Are you related to everyone here??" Back home Leila asked Mom the same question. She said, "Yes, I had one cookie. It tasted terrible, but I was so hungry."

Leila Jane learned from the caretaker that her "pot cookie" dosage was to break off a tiny corner of a cookie when needed. Three whole cookies would be a massive overdose. Indeed, Pops spent five days in the ICU recovering from this incident.

Mom and Pops

Leila's friends will not let her forget the time she got
her parents stoned. •

Beth Bixby Davis was born in Northern New York and moved
to the Asheville area of North Carolina in the mid-1960s where she
reared her family, raised Arabian horses and had a 30-year career
in nursing. Enjoying a long-time hobby of writing, she recently
published a book of short stories, essays, and poetry, called
Patchwork Collection. Her creative nonfiction work has appeared
in *Bearing Up*, *Exploring*, and *Luck and Opportunity*. She belongs
to Talespinners Writers Group.

That Bluetick Hound

by Paula Teem Levi

When I was growing up in Gastonia, North Carolina, our family went each spring to visit my grandparents in Elkins, West Virginia. One of my fondest memories is when I was 10 years old. I met a gangly, 3-year-old bluetick hound, appropriately enough, named Blue. He had a dark blue coat, thickly mottled with black spots on his back, ears, and sides. He had brown spots over his eyes and on his cheeks.

My grandfather, Omer Bennett, instructed me not to pet this dog. He said Blue was a hunter, first and foremost, not a pet. So, I watched him from afar.

In the morning, my grandmother, Bertha, went out to the chicken coop to wring the necks of some chickens for our dinner. Grandmother stretched out those necks and then spun them almost like twisting a jump rope. Blue ran after those ol' headless chickens, as they tottered and flopped across the yard. I could not help but laugh. I watched him trailing after one hen and then the other. It was quite a sight to behold.

Blue dutifully retrieved one and then the other hen for my grandmother. He placed them at her feet with pride.

That afternoon, a young black bear cub came into the yard. I was watching from the front porch. Blue started chasing after and taunting the cub. I knew a mother bear had to be nearby. I started clapping my hands and yelling at Blue to come back and to leave that cub alone. Blue had a stubborn streak, and he completely ignored me.

I barely caught a glimpse of that big mama bear as she came charging through the front yard to protect her baby. She appeared to come out of nowhere. That hound was in big trouble. Blue was no match for Mama Bear.

I ran inside to get my grandfather. Out of breath, I could hardly speak, but was finally able to tell him to come quickly to save Blue from the wrath of that mother bear. Grandfather hurriedly took a shotgun from a cabinet located next to the front door. He scurried out the door, and I followed. He fired the shotgun into the air. My ears were ringing from the impact of the shot.

Grandfather and I saw Mama Bear pick up Blue and shake him violently before she threw him through the air. He landed on the ground with a thud. Scared and screaming, I just knew that hound dog was dead. Blue lay real still for some time. Mama Bear and her cub shuffled on out of the yard. Only then did Grandfather go down the front steps to check Blue's condition.

Grandfather picked up that dog and brought him onto
the porch. He said, "The wind's been knocked out of Blue."
He summoned my grandmother to bring him a blanket,
clean towels, warm soapy water, Raleigh's Salve, and bandages.

Blue moaned with a long, drawn-out howl, baying and bawling.
He had blood coming out of the top of his head, and his left
ear was in shreds from the impact of that mother bear's paw.
Grandfather, with his weathered and calloused hands, gently
wrapped Blue in the blanket. He applied pressure with the
towel to both sides of the bleeding ear flap for several minutes,
cleaned the wounds with the soapy water, and applied salve
to the injuries. He placed a bandage on Blue's head and
bandaged the ear against his head to keep him from any
further shaking or damage. An unspoken trust flowed between
my grandfather and that dog. Blue would look at Grandfather
with those pleading, dark brown eyes. He dutifully listened
to my grandfather's commands to stay still and remain calm.

Blue was moved into the house beside the fire to keep him
warm. Grandfather did not want Blue to exert himself through
the night, following any good scents. Grandmother had boiled
the hens for chicken and dumplings. She gave Blue some
of the chicken broth to drink. He lapped it down, then settled
down for the night. Grandfather stayed in the chair next
to that dog all night. Next morning, Blue was limping around
some inside the house; but seemed to be no worse for wear.
He ate a good breakfast and, not accustomed to staying inside,
was ready to go back outside.

That Bluetick Hound

107

Blue lived to be 12 years old. To my knowledge, he never had another encounter with a mother bear. He did carry some scars from his troubles that spring day and probably a healthy respect. Blue developed cataracts in his later years and was not able to hunt as much, but he could see well enough to remain—as he always had been—a loyal and faithful friend to my grandfather. •

Paula Teem Levi is a retired Registered Nurse living in Clover, South Carolina. She is a member of several genealogical societies.
Her stories, "Broken Branch," "You Got You Another One," and "Bury Me With My People," appeared in 2019, 2020, and spring 2021 anthologies of the Personal Story Publishing Project.
Her goal is to preserve as many family stories as possible for future generations so that they will not be at risk of being forgotten or lost forever.

What Happened to Judah Quinn?

by Lois Elizabeth Hicks

It happened so quickly.

Our family gathered for a late lunch at Fuddruckers in Greensboro, North Carolina. With me were my son Daniel, his wife Amy, and grandsons, 4-year-old Noah, and 2-year-old Judah Quinn. While Dan ordered burgers, Amy claimed seats in a booth that provided a view of the dining area, the exits, and "Machine Shack," an amusement area, a safe place for children to play—or so we thought.

Noah and Judah wanted to explore the Machine Shack, so we let them go, knowing the area was enclosed. They studied their favorite game, a 7-foot high, black and yellow box decorated with cartoon characters—a "Toy Taxi." It had flashing yellow-gold lights and a red-lettered sign reading, "50¢ To Play—Good Luck."

Judah stood on tiptoe beside his big brother, both boys coveting the stuffed-critter prizes heaped inside the acrylic tower of the machine: blue elephants, pink pigs, black-and-white penguins.

Motioning for the boys to return to us, their father promised, "You can play after we eat."

Noah and Judah quickly ate and raced back over to the Toy Taxi. Soon Noah returned. "May I have a penguin now?"

Judah did not echo his brother's request because Judah had not followed Noah back to our booth.

"I need to check on Judah," Amy said as she slid from the booth. She looked around and peered between the machines, then called, "He's not here." She turned an anxious face toward us and headed toward the front of the almost empty restaurant, calling her toddler's name. Dan hurried to check the restrooms.

Judah could not have left without our seeing him—or could he?

Panicked, I ran outside, calling Judah's name, wondering if he had slipped outside the restaurant. I looked toward busy Wendover Avenue, but no little boy in a bright red shirt disturbed the flowing traffic.

I rushed to peek inside a nearby parked Chevy and I scanned the almost empty parking lot, so easily accessible to an abductor wanting to snatch a toddler. But no Judah appeared, and I heard no child's cry or wail. Fear for my grandson gripped me. Desperate, incoherent prayers for Judah's protection and safe return flew from my heart.

I re-entered the restaurant and saw Amy, pale and frightened, repetitively searching, punching 911 on her mobile while Daniel, concern marking his face, talked with management.

Frantic, I turned to rejoin Judah's frightened parents. Out of the corner of my right eye, I saw a movement of bright red. It was inside the acrylic tower of the Toy Taxi. I turned to look more closely. In a flash, I comprehended. Judah was *inside* the game machine!

There he was, waist deep in stuffed critters, holding a black-and-white penguin in his right hand and a pink pig in his left, completely absorbed in his choice.

Giddy with relief, I yelled, "Judah's in the toy case!"

Amy raced toward the Machine Shack with Daniel close behind. We gathered around the game machine, admiring its biggest prize. We were teary-eyed with relief and laughing with joy, thanking God for the safety of our troublesome toddler.

Our relief quickly turned to concern as we asked the question: How did he get in there? And, more important, how do we get him out?

"Put two quarters in," someone joked.

Daniel went to find the manager and told him, "You need to unlock the Toy Taxi because my little boy is inside the tower."

"No way," the manager replied, disbelieving, as he followed Daniel to the Machine Shack. He did not have a key to open the game.

But Judah's mother had the solution. Amy knelt beside the Toy Taxi, stretched her arm shoulder-deep up through a low trap door, grabbed a small foot and gently pulled Judah feet-first through the small opening located less than a foot above

What Happened to Judah Quinn?

the floor. It was a small door hidden from the view of grown-ups, but invitingly obvious to a toddler.

Minutes later, the manager approached the booth where we sat, exhilarated with relief.

"Is he all right?" asked the manager.

"He's okay, but disappointed that he didn't get a penguin," said Daniel.

"He should have grabbed one while he was in there," joked the manager.

As we left the restaurant, Daniel inserted two quarters into the Toy Taxi and manipulated the mechanical arm over a black-and-white penguin, but the coins fell into the return slot. He could not snag a penguin. But that was okay, too.

We already had the best prize to take home. •

Lois Elizabeth Hicks lives in rural Randolph County. Lois—a wife, mother, and grandmother—worked as a high school teacher and school media coordinator for many years while providing hands-on full care for an adult son paralyzed with quadriplegia after a spinal cord injury. During those years she joined a 5-member Winston-Salem writing group and began journal entries of caregiving and respite day's events. She now writes nonfiction stories based on those journal events. "What Happened to Judah Quinn?" occurred during one respite day.

How a Four-syllable Poem Saved My Life

by Jim Lutzweiler

The four syllables "Go Low and Slow" once saved my life. I could not pick out the poet who recited them to me from a police lineup today or even a half-century ago, when I first heard them. I seriously doubt that he or she (my flight instructor was a woman) had a degree in English literature, and I absolutely doubt that the performer possessed a Pulitzer Prize in any field. But those three syllables of assonance did more for me than any Pulitzer Prize-winner ever did with a poem or any other achievement—if keeping me alive qualifies for that characterization.

I was once a private pilot. I still am but I haven't flown recently. I almost never flew again after getting myself caught in a blinding snowstorm in which I dared not do a 180-degree turn because I had no idea what was behind me. Did I already say that visibility was pitiful? And by pitiful, I mean non-existent.

I was flying in Minnesota at the time. Minnesota is not only "the land of 10,000 lakes," as its license plates hawk. (It actually has 18,000 lakes not counting Garrison Keillor's Lake

Wobegon.) But it has somewhere between 10,000 and 18,000-quadrillion snowflakes. "White out" is one two-syllable synonym for those flakes when they decide to hold a family reunion. They did one day when I was flying back to Minneapolis from a small town in the southwestern part of the state, where I had flown my small plane on business.

Heading back north toward home, a blinding snowstorm that somehow missed the weather forecasters suddenly swept down on me. Just like that I was in the soup. In Minnesota, "soup" is often a synonym for "snow." Frightened out of what wits I had not already foolishly spent in my youth, I did the one thing that poet told me to do: "Go low and slow."

I slowed and dropped as low as I dared to keep any high-reaching radio towers from involuntarily joining up with my cockpit instruments. Fortunately, I soon spotted a 4-lane highway I recognized. I knew if I followed it at low altitude, I would not hit anything except maybe another airplane as lost as I was. The good news was this highway led right to my home airport. The bad news was that when I got within five miles of the airport, I lost sight of it. Back to what happened then momentarily.

While flying back home, I contacted the airport tower for instructions. At the same time, I looked for a landing place in case things got worse. In a few minutes I spotted a road on which I felt I could land, if necessary. The tower told me to circle around that road and wait for other instructions. Then they added an ominous codicil. Codicils usually belong on wills, not radio transmissions. But when you see the

Grim Reaper staring you in the face, simple flight instructions take on the character of codicils. What he said was: "Zero Nine Sierra, stay put for now. We have IFR pilots in trouble."

Whoa! IFR means "instrument-rated." Read that "far more skilled than me." So, I stayed put for a few minutes. Then I saw ice beginning to build up on my wings. That means you will land whether you want to or not. So, I told the tower. Then I declared for Special VFR (visual flight rules). That, in essence, is screaming "Mayday!"

The tower told me to come on in, following Highway 169. So, I did. Short of the airport I lost sight of the road. Fortunately, by then they had me on radar. As I continued flying north, I heard the tower say, "Zero Nine Sierra, don't you think you should turn east about now?"

When I turned to the right, I spotted the strobe lights from the airport. How in the world strobe lights can penetrate fog from three miles away, I do not know, but I saw them and flew to them. In a matter of minutes, I landed. And for three days, I shook.

I had a passenger with me during all this, an old college classmate. Unbeknownst to me he was experiencing vertigo. He thought we were flying upside down. I did not observe him doing this at the time, but when we first entered the snow, he had taken out his pocketknife and began tossing it in the air to see if it came down. He was wise not to distract me at the time with stupid questions like "Are we going to make it?"

We did, of course, by following the mantra "Go Low and Slow," still my favorite poem. •

James Lutzweiler is a REALTOR®, a reader, and a writer. Readers have compared him to Erasmus, Mencken, Mark Twain, and Lassie. His readers include Jimmy Carter, Terry Sanford, Robert Goulet, and God. He has written an expensive coffee-table art/poetry book entitled *The Ballad of Salvation Bill by Robert Service*; 18 chapters in a book entitled *Churchfails*; one about "The Yellow Rose of Texas"; another about the first transcontinental railroad as the major cause of the American Civil War; and, finally, one entitled *On Keeping My Mouth Shut in Sunday School.*

Grandma Troubles

by Tanya E. E. E. Schmid

When my Scandinavian grandmother turned 82, my Aunt Sharon suggested she give up driving, but Grandma would not hear of it. Shortly thereafter, with her foot accidentally on the gas instead of the brake, my grandmother launched her car into a telephone pole along the local grocery store parking lot. Two store employees carefully disentangled her from the airbag and helped her out of the car. The store manager brought her a chair and sat with her until the ambulance arrived. He told Sharon that Grandma never stopped smiling. Her upper body was bruised and sore, but she suffered no serious injuries.

"Best thing that happened to me all week," Grandma told Sharon. "That store manager is awfully handsome!" Soon as she could, Grandma baked him some cookies.

At age 86, despite my aunt's warnings and threats, Grandma secretly climbed the old ladder propped against the cherry tree in her backyard. Like a picky shopper, she reached with her parchment-skin hands and carefully selected the ripest, sweetest fruit, just as she'd done for over 50 years.

Grandma Troubles

My aunt discovered her up in the tree when she stopped by
to pick up Grandma's dirty laundry—laundry which my grandmother had already washed and ironed herself.

"Why didn't you call me? I told you I'd pick those cherries
for you!" Aunt Sharon called.

"Well, you're so busy, and they're ripe now. No use waiting
till the birds get 'em."
"Mother, that's it. I warned you."

The next day two men from the garden center in LaCrosse
showed up and cut down my grandmother's beloved cherry
tree with her watching on silently, her lips pressed tightly
together.

The following week, my aunt caught Grandma atop that same
ladder, this time washing the living room's picture window.

"Mother! Lord's sake!"
"Well, you've got better things to do."

That was the last time my grandmother saw that ladder.

When I stopped by to pick her up for church a couple of
weeks later, Grandma was on a different ladder, taking down
an enormous box from high on the shelves in her garage.

"Halloween decorations. Don't go tellin' Sharon," she winked.
"And run this ladder over to Wilma's garage before she misses
it."

"She doesn't know you borrowed it?" I asked disbelieving.

TROUBLE

"She's the one who called Sharon on me that time I cleaned the windows."

Grandma couldn't cook worth a darn, always burnt the meat and over-salted the gravy, but she had the most beautiful garden, with corn, squash, carrots, and a long row of raspberry bushes. Everyone vied for her somewhat-runny raspberry jam. That year, Sharon didn't get any.

"Mother," Sharon asked as we all gathered in the kitchen for my cousin's birthday, "got any raspberry jam for me?"

"Nope. All gone. I got some canned cherries," she said, without looking up from the burning pork chops.

Sharon also got none of Grandma's famous gladiolas that year. They decorated Wilma's porch instead. I guess Wilma found out about the borrowed ladder.

Grandma teared up every time she mentioned my grandfather, yet she blossomed after he died in his 70s. She finally had time for long-kept hobbies like quilting. For years she won blue ribbons for quilting at the Wisconsin State Fair. She sewed a large patchwork quilt every year, giving one to each of her seven grandchildren, her two sons, and even my mother— who she never much liked because she wasn't of Norwegian heritage.

"When am I going to get one, Mother?" I heard Sharon ask as they washed the dishes.

"Oh, I've got one planned for you. It's comin' along."

Grandma Troubles

That Christmas, Aunt Sharon unpacked a most beautiful patchwork quilt with branches of a lush cherry tree spreading across it.

Grandma never took medication, except during her final weeks. She had been dying of cancer for over a decade after the doctor had told her "since you've refused chemo and radiation, two years max." At age 98, Grandma's only regret was that she had not made it to 100. But we had already thrown her a big party when she turned 96. Even Wilma came.

During her last few days, she again refused pain medication, saying, "I'm past all that now. I finally get to meet my maker and I don't want to miss it just 'cause you've got me all doped up."

Aunt Sharon was there when Grandma passed. "She died smiling and naming all her sisters and brothers, friends and family that she saw come to pick her up!" Sharon said proudly.

Years later now, my aunt still gets teary any time she speaks of my grandmother—"despite," she offers, "all the trouble." •

Tanya Elizabeth Egeness Epp Schmid of the Taste Life Twice Writers was a Doctor of Oriental Medicine until 2014 when she started a permaculture farm. Her work has appeared in *Valparaiso Fiction Review*, *Sky Island Journal*, *Canary Literary Magazine*, *Whistling Shade*, *Flash Fiction Magazine*, and others. Tanya was long-listed in Pulp Literature's 2021 Flash Fiction Contest. Her work has appeared in *Poet's Choice Global Warming Anthology*, and *Quillkeeper's Summer Solstice Anthology 2021*. She is a teacher of Kyudo (Zen archery) and the author of "Tanya's Collection of Zen Stories." A native of Wisconsin, she now lives in Ascona, Switzerland. www.tanyaswriting.com

Averting an International Incident

by Marie Mitchell

I'm riding on the crowded Moscow Metro with 25 other Kentuckians touring the Soviet Union in 1987. As an American journalist I'm a little paranoid about drawing attention to myself.

But I sense someone is watching me. I discreetly glance around, searching for a sinister KGB agent cleverly disguised as a commuter. But there are no suspicious characters in sight. Just a young boy sitting quietly by his mother. He's staring at my purse. After a while he nudges his mom, points in my direction and cries, "Police."

All eyes are now on me. My heart skips a beat. What have I done to warrant calling the police? Then I realize the boy is pointing at a decorative button I'd attached to my purse. The one with a picture of the rock star, Sting, who performs with his band, The Police. Apparently, the group is popular in the Soviet Union.

As a goodwill gesture, I unhook the button and pin it on the boy's jacket. He smiles. His mother rummages through her overstuffed handbag and offers me a pair of red earrings in exchange. Whew! An international incident averted. What a relief!

Before leaving on vacation, my friends had teased me about doing something stupid and being detained or "disappeared" for it. They started calling dibs on my more treasured possessions. How absurd, I thought—then.

I figured the metro misunderstanding was the worst thing that would happen during our two weeks of travels. Wishful thinking, because a few days later . . .

I woke up early one morning in Baku, a port town that is the capital of Azerbaijan. I was wide awake and restless. So, I decided to go for a walk before breakfast. I grabbed my Nikon camera and set out on my own.

Not far from our hotel, I spotted a "babushka," a grandmotherly-type woman wearing a traditional headscarf tied under her chin. She was sweeping the sidewalk in front of her shop, using an old-fashioned, coarse-bristled broom. I held up my camera and nodded at her. She did not seem to object. So, I braced myself to steady the heavy zoom lens and adjusted the focus.

Just then a motorcycle cop spied me. And evidently did not like what he saw. He made a U-turn, and parked next to where I was crouched. He reached for my camera, expecting me to hand it over. I hesitated. But he insisted. So, I reluctantly surrendered it to him, puzzled about what crime I'd committed.

He radioed headquarters, and we stood there a long while, awkwardly staring at each other in silence. He didn't speak English. I didn't speak Russian. And no one in the small crowd we had attracted could interpret for us. So, I didn't know what I'd done wrong.

Our tour leader had warned us not to take pictures at airports, ports, or military installations. But my camera wasn't aimed at any of those sensitive spots.

Periodically I showed the officer my hotel card and tried to explain I was simply an American tourist out for an innocent stroll. No response. Until eventually he shook his head and held up his hand to silence me.

A worrisome and uncomfortable 30 minutes later, a police car arrived. The additional officers motioned for me to climb inside. I refused—pointing to my camera. I was not leaving without it. Grudgingly, the motorcycle cop placed it in the front seat, and me in the back.

I repeated my hotel's name like a mantra. Miraculously, we drove directly there. Once inside, the officers tried to usher me into a back room. Not a good sign. Fortunately, some of my group members were lounging in the lobby, and I made a beeline for them, pouring out my troubles as quickly as I could. They called Natasha, our 20-something native interpreter, to straighten things out.

Natasha rolled her eyes in disbelief when the officer explained his complaint. He was worried that the photograph of a common laborer would end up on the front page of an American newspaper or magazine, and he did not think the picture would be very flattering. He felt Baku had better scenic sites for the world to see.

The officers took down my name, room number, and departure date, but there was no further intimidation.

I felt awful about Natasha getting chewed out over the debacle, but she shrugged it off. Fortunately, the remaining stops in Tbilisi and Leningrad were remarkable, but uneventful.

After we returned home, I actually did publish an article about my adventures, with plenty of pictures included. Ironically, none were of the notorious shopkeeper. The cop must have distracted me before I could click the shutter. The upsetting image was never captured on film.

All that drama for nothing. •

After 24 years as News Director of public radio station WEKU in Richmond, Kentucky, Marie Mitchell switched to teaching at Eastern Kentucky University. She's written a column for The Richmond Register since 2007, collaborates on short stories and novels with her husband, Mason Smith, and other EKU professors (under the penname Quinn MacHollister) and meddles in the lives of her four fascinating children.

Despite the Baku debacle, Marie still enjoys traveling abroad and hosting international students at home. Her family is relieved that she has caused no further incidents overseas.

Unexpected Lessons
by Howard Pearre

M̲r. Rousseau saw me glance at the dozen tattered copies, front covers torn off, of the classic *Everything You Always Wanted To Know About Sex (But Were Afraid To Ask)* on the trailer-classroom bookshelf.

"I'm not supposed to, but I lend them out to my students," he told me. "Otherwise, they'll learn it from their friends, and that can lead to unfortunate consequences."

I had completed the requirements for a bachelor's degree in history at UNC Charlotte and was tacking on an extra semester for a teacher's certificate. I'd absorbed all the in-class instruction Dr. (Sister) Mary Thomas Burke's team had to offer. Now, I only needed to complete three months of student-teaching at Independence High School in eastern Mecklenburg County.

I was assigned to Mr. Odis Rousseau. He would oversee my instructing teenagers four periods a day about Black history and sociology. I watched his personal, quasi-counseling approach in the classroom for a week and realized I could not match his knowledge or wisdom. I had taken one sociology course a few years before and never one in Black history. But with no shortage of gumption, I figured I could just read a couple of chapters ahead of the students and roll. Little did I know.

Things were happening in Charlotte in 1972 that would affect my little classroom world in ways I failed to appreciate. The Charlotte-Mecklenburg school system, along with many other Southern school systems, had dragged its feet implementing the Supreme Court's 1954 decision in Brown v. Board of Education to desegregate public schools. Sixteen years later, U.S. District Judge James McMillan, who lived in Charlotte, had become impatient with the slow pace of implementation and ordered that system to begin busing thousands of students to achieve immediate desegregation. His order, as Bob Woodward in *The Brethren* attributed to Justice Potter Stewart, "put the Court on the spot." In 1971, after much internal contention, the Supreme Court unanimously upheld the busing order. Flight to the suburbs no longer would be an option for white parents who feared integration. Heated arguments filled school board meetings. Judge McMillan was burned in effigy and subjected to death threats.

Mr. Rousseau, a large Black man highly respected by Black and white students alike, was called on to perform duties more important in those tense times than hand-holding a novice teacher. In an era before assistant principals roamed the halls, Mr. Rousseau served at Independence in that capacity without the title. I rarely saw Mr. Rousseau after my first week. When I did, it was usually in the halls as he directed traffic and calmed waters with a warm smile and a rolling laugh that resonated all the way from the cafeteria entrance to the gym lobby.

While my classroom was never the scene of direct conflict, there was underlying tension. The Black history classes were comprised primarily of Black students along with a handful of white students, most of whom sat together in small bunches. The white students arrived via school buses or cars from the rural parts of the county, and the Black students rode buses from inner-city Charlotte. Many of the Fords and Chevies in the student parking lot were adorned with Confederate flag commemorative plates. That the white students had signed up for the class thinking they would be studying Confederate history presented additional challenges. One day in an attempt to enhance learning, I allowed a student to play a recording I had not prescreened about the "Black experience." Some of the white students walked out, and I wound up having to write an apology to their parents.

Otherwise, I was able to stay ahead of the students, administer pop quizzes, and stick to lesson plans. I learned some high-school-level Black history and that day-to-day teaching is a tough path. Near graduation, I began seeking employment with school systems in two states, but a job market flooded with new social studies teachers, and the fact that I still had some GI Bill left, convinced me to go in another direction.

When I reflect on my experiences as a student teacher, I have a much greater appreciation now of the role my mentor Mr. Rousseau was playing in that volatile time. Likewise,

I recognize the courage of Judge McMillan in forcing the hand of the Supreme Court, whether or not busing achieved its intended goals. I also understand that the stress I felt trying to maintain order in the classroom and to teach academic material to teenagers was small compared with the stress the teenagers were feeling, having been drafted into an intractable social justice struggle not of their making. •

Howard Pearre received an "early out" from the Army in 1969. He returned to UNC Charlotte for a degree in history and later attended Appalachian State University for a degree in rehabilitation psychology. He is retired after a career with North Carolina Vocational Rehabilitation as a counselor and manager and with the Department of Veterans' Affairs as a counselor. He received an honorable mention for a short story "September, 1957" at the 2020 International Human Rights Arts Festival and is a member of Winston-Salem (North Carolina) Writers.

Sex Equations

by Mary Clements Fisher

The Sixties sexual revolution never made the headlines at my house. Neither did the FDA's approval of the pill buried in the back pages of the state newspaper. But without fail, Mama's "Sex = Pregnancy = Trouble" briefing at our kitchen table every Saturday happened right alongside the cleaning to-do list.

How-to and why-to never entered our discussions. Mama and my older sister Liz confused me with their hushed conversations until I spied a sex education book on our living room corner bookcase. Later I discovered Papa (also Reverend Clements) offered this book with his counsel and blessing to engaged couples before marriage. Curiosity about sex felt akin to sin, so I hunched in a swivel chair with my back to passersby and pored over the line drawings and dry definitions. *What* appeared in black and white on the pages. *How* one would ever get into those awkward positions, *why* one would, and *where* remained mysteries until I found my *whom*.

How my parents or parishioners in the pews would manage the diagramed poses distressed me. Under what circumstances

would I ever get naked with the boy who smiled at me
in homeroom? With my flat chest and in my Lollipop three-
pair-for-a-dollar cotton panties, I undressed huddled behind
my gym locker door. Nakedness made me stress sweat.

Even more perplexing, where would such a complicated event
take place? Not at my house. Not at his. Not in the woods
with chigger bites on my bottom or poison oak in unspeakable
places. Cars presented the most dangerous venue to our virtue,
Mama warned. A neighbor boy picked her up on the way home
from country school, pulled off on a side road, and rolled over
on her until she threatened him with her three brothers. Mama
often said, "Eve wasn't the problem; Adam ate the apple."
Sex in a backseat, in a motel room, or on a slab tombstone—
Mama didn't have to worry, but she did for years.

My sister Liz left for college. She'd passed the test of Mama's
lessons by not dating until a friend's owlish cousin took her
to senior prom. Even in college, her espoused equation
remained stark: "Avoid Boys = Avoid Trouble." Avoidance
didn't work for me. Sex education talks resumed when I got
my period at 15. Mama then focused all her "Sex = Trouble"
fears on me. Her deterrents emerged from tales of girls
disgraced. She pursed her lips, wiped away a tear, and
bemoaned, "The poor thing drove her ducks to a bad market,"
an adage echoed throughout my mother's upbringing. "Driving
my ducks" meant ruining Papa's pastoral reputation and
Mama's and derailing my life forever. Gossip about backroad
sexual escapades ran rampant in my rural high school,
so I shied away from situations which might raise salacious
speculations and scandalize my family.

TROUBLE

To her credit, Mama organized church-sponsored baby showers, suffered with the sullied girls, and squashed gossip. "Don't go talking about her beyond these kitchen walls. Stand with her. She'll need friends now more than ever." Dear Mama didn't believe pregnancy was catching.

With Mama's tutelage, I internalized the shame and pain too many girls felt and became an ambassador to the fallen. My senior year, one of my best friends got pregnant. Uncharitable girls derided her with "She asked for it" nonsense. Crude boys pointed at her double-D breasts and insulted her with sucking noises.

I spat my threat with eyes ablaze, "What would your mothers and my father say if they heard your venomous talk?" The scolded snakes slithered away for the moment, but bitten and battered, my friend dropped out of school. Her boyfriend stayed and graduated. His parents resisted his pleas to let him marry her until they saw the baby with his red hair and green eyes. Two divergent formulas emerged: "Boys + Sex = Little Trouble," but "Girls + Sex = BIG Trouble." Thank goodness my research and experiences in college provided me an improved personal equation.

The boy who smiled at me back in junior high homeroom became my significant *whom*. Though we attended different universities, we plotted our weekends and futures together. My affection and passion for him persuaded me to take the pill and buy sex-appealing underwear. William's apartment provided the privacy we desired. Mama never asked me questions when we visited home, but she noticed my quick-

Sex Equations

ening breath and rising blush when William brushed my leg. With one eyebrow raised, she sighed, "You're in love."

My birth control confidence, my dedication to my degree, and the depth of William's and my love persuaded Mama to accept—if not celebrate—my sex life. She quit worrying only after I graduated with honors and married William, a man she'd grown to love, too.

I recommend:
Love + Maturity + Protection + Sex = No Trouble at All. •

Mary Clements Fisher enjoyed her careers as an educator and businesswoman and still celebrates her mother/grandmother status. She lives with her sweetheart of over fifty years in Northern California and takes psychology and writing courses at Stanford University. A member of Taste Life Twice Writers, she writes about women's and children's trials and triumphs and is published in *Quail Belle Magazine, Adanna Journal's Fall 2020 Issue, Passager Journal's Pandemic Diaries,* and *The Weekly Avocet #450.* @maryfisherwrites

Water Lessons

by Landis Wade

When I was a toddler, my mother tried to kill me. She took me to the YMCA and handed me to a half-dressed devil of a man with aged and leathered skin. He threw me in the deep end of the pool and laughed. He called it "swimming lessons." The only lesson I took from the experience was to kick and scream every time Mom tried to take me back, and to this day, when I whiff that bleach-like scent from a chlorine infested indoor pool, it all comes floating back.

As a young boy, I didn't understand why Mom wasn't satisfied to let me play in the sprinkler. It was just as wet and just as cool. My playmates, whose mothers tried to murder them too, agreed. And because we liked the idea of playing in water that wasn't over our heads, we took to splashing around in the neighborhood creeks. All went well until the biggest snake this side of the Amazon tried to eat my buddies and me. I swear the snake chased us 50 feet, and to this day, I am skeptical of the rule that if you leave a snake alone, it will ignore you.

It should be no surprise that when Mom asked me if I wanted to be on the swim team, I declined. Swimming made me think of that devil who tried to drown me. I also didn't like the fact you couldn't touch the bottom during the race. By sticking to land sports, I avoided competitive swimming until a pretty girl smiled and asked me to fill in on her high school relay team at the local pool. "Just do freestyle." I did and swam hard. It was a neck and neck race until the lump of ignorance my neck held in place slammed into the wall at the half-way mark. When I stood up to check the damage, they disqualified me in my first and last swim meet. The effort did not impress the pretty girl, and to this day, when I hear the starter's gun pop at the neighborhood pool, my head aches a little.

As high school seniors close to graduation, my friends and I gave special meaning to the phrase: "boys do stupid things in groups." We dared each other to climb to the top of the metal structure that held Buster Boyd Bridge together, 20 feet above moving traffic and 40 feet above the muddy water of Lake Wylie. Submerged pilings from the old bridge were the farthest things from our minds. We jumped to save face and lived to tell the stupid tale. But to this day, every time I cross a bridge with a superstructure, I feel the need to hold my breath.

My problem with boats began on the Cape Fear River when I was 11. Dad borrowed my uncle's Chris Craft for the 3-day journey. It sputtered and died on the watery backside of nowhere between Fayetteville and Wilmington. He later bought a small outboard he flipped in the surf while trolling for Spanish Mackerel near Mason's Inlet, and later, I lost one of Dad's boats. I'd anchored it in Banks Channel, but it drifted off one night when the wind got up. That led to a Coast Guard story I kept from Dad until we found and reanchored the boat.

In college, I was old enough to drink beer with spicy food. Dad had the idea to take me deep sea fishing with one of his friends who had a seaworthy boat. The previous night's combination of alcohol and pepperoni pizza didn't mix well with the smell of diesel and the slow rolling swells on the way to the Gulf Stream. The only thing I caught that day besides a close-up view of the head was a desire never to go deep sea fishing again.

Mom must have known what she was doing with the swimming lessons and Dad, once a beach lifeguard, took it from there. He taught me bodysurfing, and took me on motorboat rides, where we sped across coastal waterways with wind in our hair. He took me saltwater fishing as a youngster, and though it didn't take, I discovered fly-fishing in my fifties and took him along.

I've found a common denominator in saltwater surfs and waterways, freshwater trout streams and rivers, and long, hot showers—the ones without much chlorine. It's called happiness, and it's in the genes. Mom was happy she didn't have to worry about me playing in water over my head. Dad's happiness is on display in the photo I keep of him in the captain's chair of his Grady White, his last boat, where he wears a broad smile. Me? I'm happy my parents gave me lessons. They were more than worth the trouble. •

Water Lessons

Landis Wade is a recovering trial lawyer, award-winning author, and host of Charlotte Readers Podcast (charlottereaderspodcast.com), where authors give voice to their written words. His third book—The Christmas Redemption—won the Holiday category of the 12th Annual National Indie Excellence Awards. His essays, "Shelby," "Two Good Swings," "Southern Tides," and "What Luck These Friendships," appeared in *Bearing Up, Exploring, That Southern Thing, and Luck and Opportunity,* four earlier anthologies published by the Personal Story Publishing Project.

Cappie: the Boomerang Horse

by Janet K. Baxter

C appie is back home!

I bought Starbucks Iced Cappuccino (aka, Cappie) in 2006. He was a silver-dapple, 3-year-old stallion, a rare color in the Tennessee Walking Horse breed. I was developing a small-scale breeding program and found a local barn that would board and manage this young stallion. I also purchased two brood mares and a filly sired by Cappie, Taramisu. I was building my dream.

Then the national economy tanked in 2008 and 2009 and, at the same time, North Carolina suffered a series of droughts. The horse market died. Hay was difficult to find; fields lay burnt in the blistering sun. My dream quickly became a financial nightmare.

A stallion is typically kept away from other horses except for breeding. Cappie had spent most of his young life isolated in a stall, which provided no experience living in a herd. I had Cappie gelded, brought him home to my barn, and sold two of the mares. As I pondered plans for Cappie's future and after time for adjustment, Cappie was released into my middle pasture with my head mare, Missy. Like a teen bully, he tried her patience. She, however, would tolerate none of that. Missy swiftly taught him to watch her ears and mind her hind legs. Her ears gave him a warning, her hind legs drove hard the lesson.

I used the few training techniques I knew, but Cappie's behavior told on me. I didn't bond well with Cappie, so rather than keep him as my riding horse, I planned to sell him as a trail horse. However, training Cappie for trail riding was fraught with frustration and confusion on my part and perceived stubbornness and ill-behavior on his, which is not a good combination.

Finally, I sold Cappie and specifically advised the new owner that Cappie didn't like someone "yanking" on the reins to stop him. I suggested that she take riding lessons for a few months to learn riding seat and leg cues. However, only one day later, she brought him back. She had saddled him his first day in a new place and took him riding in her pasture past the neighbor's horses. When he spooked at the horses, she had difficulty controlling him and that frightened her. So, Cappie came home, again.

Unfortunately, a successful trail ride remained elusive, and I consistently chose another horse to ride for pleasure.

A few years later, I met another woman who was looking for a small, older horse. She promised to work with him, and she had someone with whom she could ride to give Cappie an experienced horse to follow. I was hopeful that Cappie found a good match, but I retained right-of-first refusal. That weekend she arrived with an old, broken-down, rust-covered trailer. Although I had wanted to reduce the size of my herd, my heart sank as I watched her drive away.

Two months later, I received a text from the new owner; her boarding situation was terminated:

> I've been asked to move Cappie! I have nowhere to go! SHE WANTS HIM GONE WITHIN THE WEEK. NEED TO DO THIS ASAP!!!

That same afternoon, I found Cappie in a small, wooded, hilly lot with rivulets of eroding brown soil and no grass. Although well fed, his too small halter was digging into his face and muzzle. I also learned that he had been used as a lesson horse for children. I was upset at his situation, but what was most surprising, overjoyed to see him. I could not load him into my trailer quickly enough. He easily adjusted back into my herd, happily soaking his hay in his water bucket and snarfing up the lush pasture grass. Cappie was home—again.

A persistent refrain of *"What do I need to learn?"* to *"What is Cappie doing or needing now?"* tickles my thoughts. I am grateful for new online options that provide access to national and international instructors and trainers. When I ride Cappie now, I notice that he resists while turning and I feel his heart racing beneath my seat with each request to slow or halt. I am revisiting ground work and in-hand work with Cappie, softly coaxing him to release this tension. I've switched bits to one that uses a pushing action. I am also fine-tuning the use

Cappie: the Boomerang Horse

of the reins and reteaching him to halt using a balance rein as an intermediate cue between the seat and the rein cues.

Best of all, and more importantly, my 14-year-old grand-daughter, Mikaela, wants Cappie for her own when she visits. I lead riding my veteran gelding while Cappie and Mikaela follow on the trail providing Cappie the experience he needs.

Cappie is here to stay. •

Janet K. Baxter lives in Kings Mountain, North Carolina, and is a member of the Charlotte Writer's Club and Scribblers, a memoir critique group. Her stories "Horse Whispering for the Average Woman" appeared in *Exploring* (2019), "Southern Blues" appeared in *That Southern Thing* (2020) and "A Frank Lesson" appeared in *Luck and Opportunity* (2021) from the Personal Story Publishing Project. Janet enjoys her seven grandchildren and all the critters that populate her "mini-estate." Pictures of Cappie and her granddaughter's first trail ride can be found on Cappie's page at: www.mountaingaitacres.com.

Bad Boys

by Jane Satchell McAllister

At my mother's memorial service, I spoke about her nurturing spirit and the miracle of our parents raising, on a minister's salary, four rowdy sons and one perfect daughter. The gathering laughed at that unexpected moment of levity, which revealed an important truth about our upbringing—we survived by parental grace.

As the middle child of five, I grew up well positioned to observe the antics of my compatible two older brothers and the feuding younger brothers. The succession of troublesome situations, major and minor, into which my brothers fell seemed unending.

At my father's first church on the Eastern Shore of Maryland, the congregation held a welcome reception on the pier extending into the Chesapeake Bay, with my father wearing his new suit for the occasion. My elder brothers, Bob and Dick, tussled. Dick fell into the bay and my father jumped in after him, saving Dick but ruining the suit. The Satchell family made its mark with that church early on.

Bob and Dick embraced the cowboy-and-Indian popular culture of their childhoods in the 1950s. One day, Bob persuaded his cowboy gang to stage a hanging, volunteering Dick as the "hangee." As Dick tells it, once dangling with legs off the ground, he squeaked out a protest and, thankfully, was lowered to safety.

As a teen working to earn pocket money, Dick experienced a too-close encounter with a machete while cutting weeds, resulting in his thumb hanging by a thread. Mom raced him to the hospital where the surgeon miraculously reattached the thumb. As a registered nurse, Mom consistently responded to our medical emergencies calmly and competently.

While Bob honed his entrepreneurial skills by buying bulk candy and selling individual pieces at a profit to his fellow students, Dick practiced chemistry. Apparently, the benzene fire in the high school chemistry lab was not quite as bad as the rocket fuel experiment in a friend's kitchen.

Forsythia bushes featured prominently in our childhood years. As if the spanking itself was not bad enough, as my youngest brother John recalls, our mother insisted that the boys choose their own switches. Mom did not tolerate any of the boys choosing a skinny flimsy branch.

As a child, John required significant reconstructive surgery on his upper lip after being bitten by a neighbor's dog. Several years thereafter, while riding his bike, he upended himself over the handlebars and landed on his face, destroying the good results of the surgery.

As preacher's kids, we rarely missed Sunday worship services, though sometimes my younger brothers forgot where we were. They were acting up during Dad's sermon one Sunday, disturbing members of the congregation. Mid-sentence, my father halted his sermon and announced, in his deep booming voice, "Will and John, if you do not behave, I will come down there and escort you out of this building." Truly, you could have heard a pin drop in that sanctuary for the remainder of the service.

Tasked with finding and summoning John home for dinner, Will discovered him happily ensconced in a friend's treehouse. His entreaties resolutely ignored, Will resorted to warfare. He hurled a rock at John and, beyond all odds, hit John in the head, leaving a knot Will's victim claims he still has, to prove it.

The principal's office at the junior high school John attended called Mom. Frustrated with his Spanish teacher, he had commented disparagingly including a few English cuss words, thereby earning a spell in detention, yet again. My mom's face fell as she listened on the phone and then related the news to me. Both of us remained appropriately somber for a moment, then burst into hilarious laughter. That boy!

On a family trip to Disney World, John and I rode Space Mountain. It was John's first—and last—roller coaster ride. The experience so terrified him that at the end of the ride, his hands remained frozen on the safety bar for a full 10 minutes.

Given the trail of disturbances with the boys, my minor transgressions paled by comparison. My single trip to the principal's

Bad Boys

office resulted from boredom in music class, my remedy
for which was shredding notebook paper into tiny pieces
and releasing them over the air vent behind my seat,
providing a brief but enjoyable shower of confetti.

As adults, all five siblings returned to the Eastern Shore
to celebrate our parents' wedding anniversary. For a family
outing, we paddled canoes on the Pocomoke River which led
to an "accidental" collision with our parents' boat, sending
them into the water. Both emerged grinning, re-entered the
boat, and got safely to shore. My father's glasses likely remain
embedded in the river bottom silt.

My parents loved us unconditionally, troubles included,
and we believe—says "the perfect daughter"—they would
not have had it any other way. •

Copyright 2021, Jane Satchell McAllister

Jane Satchell McAllister's writings draw inspiration from the wide
variety of people and places she encounters, from her home base
in Davie County, North Carolina to rich adventures across our
country and abroad. She has co-authored two Images of America
books through Arcadia Publishing prior to serving as the director
of the county's public library for nine years. Her current main
writing project involves compiling her family's stories so that their
descendants can better understand and enjoy their heritage.

Playing Chicken with a Snowplow

by Sharon Stegall

"**S**haron, did you drive the car anywhere else other than the high school?"

I had just made my way downstairs that morning, which meant my 18-year-old brain was barely awake. "Um, no?"

"I'm relieved to hear that," Dad answered, "but do you know how the car got an extra 50 miles on the odometer?"

I was caught! My dad looked at me for an explanation. Like any teenager, I would normally perpetuate the lie, but with the objective evidence presented, I was trapped. I opted to give him a partial truth.

I confessed that one of the weekly busses taking the ski club from the high school to the slopes 45 minutes away was late. I finessed that since I had driven my stepmom's green 1971 VW Beetle to school that day (a special privilege), I had a car. The bus was, in fact, late. And I did, in fact, offer to drive my girlfriends to Greek Peak, rather than waiting "FOR-EV-ER" (probably at least 15 minutes). That explained the excess mileage. Being a teenager automatically meant that I thought of myself as old enough to make my own decisions, so it never occurred to me to ask for permission to drive that far. I didn't even think about calling. *Sorry?*

As my dad gave me one of his infamous needing-to-know-but-glad-you-are-safe lectures, I silently relived the rest of the story from the previous afternoon.

I drove "Bug," as the car was affectionately called, from Ithaca High School on Highway 13 out of Ithaca, New York, to Greek Peak in Cortland, a place where students who had signed up for the ski club were transported every Thursday after school during the winter. My friends and I all rented our skis there, otherwise we never would have been able to consider fitting ski equipment plus three girls in a VW Bug. The ski club participants typically skied all afternoon and evening, returning to the school parking lot around 9 p.m.

Surprising or not, a lot of partying happened in the chartered buses on the way to and from Greek Peak, as well as on the slopes. This was the early '80s, when the legal drinking age was 18, the police didn't automatically lock you up if you drove under the influence, and seat belt laws were still being debated.

In the privacy of the Bug that day, it was no different although as the driver, I was not a consumer. I also was in the habit of wearing my seatbelt. This is about where my nerdiness stopped. With me in the car were my best friends, Chris and

Tracy. We chatted and laughed as we made our way through an intersection where the vehicles ahead of me were having to adjust their paths for a car which had stopped too far into the intersection approaching from the right. Still moving at a good clip, I followed the line of other cars into the left-hand lane to avoid the intruding car. As the truck directly ahead of me moved back to the right lane, it revealed what it had hidden from my view—an industrial-sized highway snowplow coming the other way straight toward us.

"Holy crap!" I yelled. I braked and pulled hard to the right. Bug went into a spin on the icy road. I hung onto the steering wheel for dear life. In the passenger seat, Chris screamed and grabbed the "oh shit" handle placed above the glove compartment of every Volkswagen Beetle. In the back seat, Tracy was frozen in position, lighting a joint. Bug spun completely around three times, missed the plow somehow, and straightened out on the other side of the intersection, sliding toward a large ditch and a pile of snow over two feet high. My mind flashed forward to a scene where my dad would tearily watch my little car being towed out of the ditch. This would give him more reasons to worry and—even worse— more lecture material for life.

Oh, hell, no! I thought as I put all my concentration and effort onto the brake pedal. Miraculously, Bug stopped just a few inches shy of the ditch. We were on the side of the road, shaken but safe. Tracy put the joint away, my friends frantically dug out their seatbelts and we made it the rest of the way to Greek Peak.

Playing Chicken with a Snowplow

I took a lot of ribbing about my driving ability and playing chicken with a snowplow until I graduated. I countered with, "Hey, maybe I should have slowed down more, but I saved your butts, didn't I? You're welcome."

Looking back, it was a miracle no one got hurt. Even better, the police were not involved, Bug wasn't damaged, and no parents ever found out . . . unless they read this story. •

Sharon Stegall has recently relocated from Connecticut to Winston-Salem, North Carolina. Without sacrificing fun and adventure, Sharon is trying to lead a less perilous life in her middle years. Her blog, *Sharon Space*, focuses on a humorous look at breeding and showing Maine Coon cats and living with other creatures, human and non-human. Sharon is a contributing author for the book *Maine Coon Cats–The Owners Guide from Kitten to Old Age*.

Chancing the Buddy System

by Patrica E. Watts

When Scott was still in high school, he and his dad took a chance on the "buddy system." They planted not just their farm but, they stretched themselves to plant substantial rented acreage, too. They had not only a wheat crop to plant and harvest but corn and cotton crops as well. They would do it together. And like most boys who grew up on a farm, Scott knew hard work was not optional. Sometimes weather put you behind, sometimes broken equipment did. You learned to work through those struggles. But there were delightful times as well where Scott and his dad could come out of the field, either get the hunting dogs and hunt quail or go fishing on those wonderful South Carolina afternoons.

But when Scott's dad was diagnosed with cancer that spring, it was more than devastating. His dad died six months later at the age of 46, with a large crop still in the field. And he left a brokenhearted young man on the tractor. Not only had Scott lost the father he loved deeply, but he was also left to get that "buddy system" crop in by himself. He worked incredibly hard,

got the crops in, paid the debts, and then parked the tractor.
He missed his dad, his buddy, terribly.

Unexpected, another opportunity soon came Scott's way—
a job on the railroad. He was fascinated with trains, always had
been. He was single; he could travel. So, he applied for the job
and was accepted. But "the times were a'changin" in the 1960s.
There were rumblings of ramping up the selective service draft
and talk of sending young men to Vietnam.

Scott's friend from a neighboring farm came to see him, asking
him to join the Air Force with him. He said they could go in
on the Buddy System and would get to stay together for the
whole enlistment. After a long discussion, the two decided they
would rather stay together than wait for the draft. They went
together to take their Air Force entrance exams. Somehow that
day Scott got off by one bubble on the answer key making the
rest of the answers down the page wrong. He would have
to take it over, but his friend decided he did not want to take
a chance of getting drafted. He enlisted on his own. Once
again Scott lost a buddy.

So, Scott continued with the railroad job until he got that
inevitable call from the draft board. He then did not have
a choice: he would have to serve. As it was, Scott liked his job
and had been promoted with the railroad. And that would be
the last job he had before being sent to Colorado for two years
to train at Fort Carson.

Scott soon found out what Army life was like living in
draughty old World War II barracks where snow came blasting

off the Rockies through the open cracks in the winter and the sand off the windy plains in the summer. He found out what training in the desert was like with hot sand pelting your face during the day and then freezing temperatures that very same night. And no way to shower. But he was a country boy; he knew about trouble. He fared better than most. And hunting quail with his dad had made him an excellent shot.

Scott had made several buddies while serving in the Army. One buddy wanted to do something special and introduce Scott to a young woman, Pat. He thought they would be a good match for each other. He was sure he could arrange for the two to meet. But the trouble was her parents had adamantly said their daughter could never date a soldier. Scott's buddy, a persistent fellow, argued his case several times. Eventually, the parents relented, consenting to just one date. After they met him, Scott certainly passed muster. He began showing up at the doorstep more frequently. He had won over the parents and Pat. After a few dates, the two discovered something almost unbelievable.

Scott's last job when he left South Carolina and was sent to Colorado was the exact same last job Pat's great-grandfather had when he left South Carolina and came to Colorado three generations earlier. Both men had been Section Foreman for The Seaboard Railroad at Carlisle, South Carolina.

What were the chances these two men would have had the exact same position with the same company, that both men would leave South Carolina, both ending up in Colorado? And what were the chances Scott would somehow meet the great granddaughter who would become his wife? It could have been coincidence, but despite all the troubles, it just might have been Scott's continuing willingness to take a chance on the Buddy System! •

Patricia E. Watts lives in Mountville, South Carolina, where the love of local and family history has given her a passion to write stories to pass down to her children. She has found through stories of tragedies, tears, and triumphs and even mysteries that she has a rich heritage worth telling. Her story "A Real Small Town" appeared in 2020 PSPP's *That Southern Thing* and her paired stories "Sometimes the Prize Goes to the Wrong Person" and "The Orphan Train" appeared in spring 2021 PSPP's *Luck and Opportunity*.

Bonneville Blues

by Patricia Cooper Baker

When the 1974 Bonneville was showroom fresh, the 2-ton gas-guzzler belonged to my stepmother, Candy. When it was no longer the best model available, she sold it to us. My husband had a new Chevy, but despite Candy's warning that the car was trouble, he forked over $600, so I could drive that "baby-safe" tank with fading blue paint.

The car came with the kids in the divorce settlement.

After my first lesson in the perils of selecting paint from a chip, and the expected "Seaside Silver" turned out to be "Robin's Egg" blue, I called it the Blue Goose. Gas attendants didn't mind. They cheered the arrival of the Blue Goose with its 8-mpg habit. It got the kids and me from A to B—if A wasn't too far from B.

On holidays when his mother was cooking, my ex-husband had the kids, and I was on my own. What does a newly single mother of three do with spare time? Single women don't fit well into the lives of long-time married friends, and the

"Robin's Egg" blue boat-on-wheels was not a date magnet. Still, I wasn't about to spend my free time moping at home. I was braver than that. And it's better to be sorry for something you do than for something you don't. But what could I do alone?

People don't notice you are alone when you have a camera in hand, so I geared up the best 35-mm rig my Sears credit card could buy. Who'd know I was ignorant of any principles of photography? Well, maybe the guy who had to tell me to take the setting off macro if I wanted my kids in focus, but not many others.

One weekend in summer 1982, I decided to snap scenery around Lake Lure, North Carolina. At the inn parking area, a guy asked me why the car had a sticker on the window touting its anti-theft alarm. Who knew? Maybe my stepmother had a sense of humor.

The following day, I found my driver's door pried open, and I traded the inn's grapes and Danish for a breakfast of repair-shop coffee. My morning reading was posters on the wall: the price of an air filter, a selection of mirror dice, and the ABCs of getting cars out of snowdrifts. *Cars We Love* was on TV when the mechanic returned.

"Everything but the door is fine," he said, "but why's this crowbar sitting on your engine?"

Oops. That anti-theft sticker made somebody think the old car was worth some trouble. Too bad the alarm didn't work. Now

I had a sprung door that wouldn't lock properly—and a free crowbar. Life goes on, and so did my photography.

Streams, bottomless pits, and distant views of the Chimney Rock were great, but what about vistas from side roads? Time for "off-roading." Remember: Better to be sorry for something you did. So, I tried the winding dirt trails. The first turn was "Cliff Cove Road." Now, I had not yet learned that if you follow any road named "Cove," you'll be coming back the same way. If you're lucky.

I wasn't.

It takes a lot of water to feed Lake Lure, and low-lying land gets its share, too. Sadly, the road headed to the underbelly of Cliff Cove instead of up to the ridges. It soon turned into a rut-filled mud marsh with barely any room to turn this big blue bus of a Bonneville.

I did it, though. Then promptly got stuck in the mud.

I could make a car go forward and back and keep it in the lanes, but I never learned anything about getting one unstuck from the mud, and I was stuck good.

All I could think of was, *Oh, My God.* It was praying, not blaspheming. *Dirty Dancing*, not *Deliverance*, was filmed in Lake Lure, but I heard the strains of "Dueling Banjos." Cliff Cove was desolate, and I did not relish knocking on strange doors.

What to do? I locked the three good doors and looked around

to find a camera, a crowbar, and a lint-covered pacifier. Panicking, I jammed the crowbar through my door handle. Then I remembered the posters from the service station. Could you get out of a mud rut the same way as out of a snowbank? Would rocking the car work?

With the crowbar holding my door in place, I shifted forward, then reverse and rocked it back and forth. Maybe I turned it a little, I don't know. But after a few back-and-forths, the old 2-ton Blue Goose kicked out of the mud, and I spun upward toward pavement.

That car was not trouble; whatever shade, it was "True Blue." And the lucky crowbar that pointed me to the snowbank poster is never far from me, even today. •

Patricia Cooper Baker lives in Maggie Valley, North Carolina, where she is a member of the Mountain Writers Coalition. She is a lifetime writer, but after teaching, consulting, and managing online communities, she now writes fulltime. The tribulations of Trish's Burke County family during the American Revolution are reflected in her *Freedom Tavern* series. Her current projects include a time-travel series *Top Shelf Tales* (pre-teen to adult) and a new Sci-fi series, *Martian Spring* (young adults and up). Read about her past and ongoing work at Cooperspeak.com.

Trick-or-Treat Or Fraud

by Maria Cloninger

It was Halloween. At 11 years old, I had outgrown trick-or-treating. Friday nights were meant to be spent hanging with my friends, swapping old issues of teen magazines, and swooning over the latest movie stars. But Halloween 1969? Not my best year. I was pressed into being in charge of five little tykes for the annual ritual. Only two of them were my sisters; the others were cousins.

Well of course I wasn't "dressing up." What if my friends saw me? Or worse, what if their brothers saw me with a bunch of babies. I could hear their snickers and taunts already. So, I decided that the only way to save my dignity was to do some charity work while I was carrying out my responsibilities as a nursemaid to a band of brats.

The night before, I had watched an episode of *Bewitched* in which Tabitha had participated in a program called "Trick-or-Treat for U.N.I.C.E.F." It was all so noble. She had a little orange box with U.N.I.C.E.F. printed in bold letters across the front. When her neighbors answered her knock, she would sweetly say: "Trick-or-Treat for U.N.I.C.E.F!" and thrust her little box out in front of her. Well, of course, it was a huge success. Not only did she get a ton of candy, but she raised a nice little piece of change for kids who really needed help. The next day, she turned the money in at school along with the rest of the kids and everybody was a hero. Now, I wasn't about to ask for candy, but I sure didn't mind asking for charity for underprivileged kids.

I found an Ivory soap box, covered it with orange construction paper and printed "U.N.I.C.E.F." in bold magic marker around the box. I cut a slit in the short edge for coins. I was very pleased with my handiwork. As dusk neared, I felt quite proud that I had decided to turn a bad situation into something really good. I gathered up my band of merry pirates, ghosts and witches and headed for the subdivision behind my family's acreage.

As luck would have it, many people had seen that episode of *Bewitched* and were thrilled to give their spare coinage for such a worthy cause. It seemed that they looked even more kindly upon my little charges and were very charitable with their candy treats also. I was thrilled, the little brats were fat and happy, and a great night was had by all. I managed to collect a total of $7.49. Now, in 1969 that was a pretty hefty chunk of change, about $50 today.

When I took my collection to school on Monday and turned it in to my teacher, she looked quite confused and had me take the money to the principal's office. There, I was informed that our county school system had not participated in this program. They actually never had. So, I was pretty much on my own.

Up the creek. No paddle. Just me and a tricked-out soap box filled with coins. I was literally sick to my stomach, afraid it would look as if I had collected the money under false pretenses. I was clammy and sweaty and as jumpy as a cat at a dog show.

I needed a plan to rectify this situation. I didn't want to get caught with the evidence of my apparent con job, so I took the money home and stuffed the offending spoils from my unintentional grift into the back of my sock drawer. Then with a thin backstory, I announced to Mom I wasn't wearing socks anymore because, uh . . . they made my feet hot. Yeah, it was stupid. But, hey, age 11. Hindsight.

But alas, my fate was sealed when Mom ran into my teacher at the grocery. The teacher asked how we had resolved "the U.N.I.C.E.F. situation." Busted. The storm broke. Thunder rolled. Mom's brand of justice was to spank first and ask questions later. Hail rained down on my behind so that I sat funny for a week. Later, satisfied that I had not intentionally set out to defraud our neighbors, she took me to buy a money order and mail it to U.N.I.C.E.F. Of course, the associated costs came out of my allowance, but my conscience was clear.

I now understood the meaning of the old saying about the road to hell being paved with good intentions, not to mention the one about "the tangled web we weave." I also learned that some meticulous planning and a little more attention to detail might have served me just as well. After all, who wants to be accused of selling their soul for $7.49—even adjusted for inflation? •

Trick-or-Treat Or Fraud

Maria Cloninger lives in Shelby, North Carolina, and enjoys partici-
pating in local writers' groups and workshops and attending book
signings to meet and talk with the authors. After years of crafting
legal briefs for federal court as a disability specialist, Maria decided
to pursue writing for pleasure. She enjoys the challenge of writing
short essays and stories. She is working on a novel based on the
interesting life of a family member.

In Trouble
by Nancy Tilly

A t the end of seventh grade in 1948, our friend Libby invited Betty and me to spend a week with her family on the Island, our Atlanta term for St. Simon's Island on the Georgia coast. Betty had a crush on Libby's older-by-two-years brother Robert, who was handsome, adventurous—and mean. Robert bragged before we left that he had some marijuana he planned to smoke. I was shocked. I'd seen the movies. Marijuana could kill you. Maybe Robert hadn't been serious.

The beach was warm, the weather sunny, and the scooter company rented scooters to 12- and 13-year-olds. We had a fine time tooting around the place. Sandy-haired Betty and I began to work on our tans. Libby's hair was dark brown, and though her eyes were blue like ours, she didn't tan and had to be careful in the sun. The Armstrongs were older parents and left us to ourselves, except for meals and a movie. Perhaps Betty and I had forgotten Robert's plan—or threat—but one evening when the Armstrongs were on the shady front porch and the four of us still lazed on the beach, Robert said, "Tonight's the night."

We girls all slept in one of the three upstairs bedrooms, and I'm sure Libby's parents expected us to talk until late, the way we always did when we spent the night with each other, which was often. Though I'd turned 13 in June, I was more child than teenager. It was beyond my understanding why Robert was planning this rendezvous with a dangerous drug. The Armstrongs were sleeping across the hall, and Robert figured he'd have the downstairs to himself.

Did Betty or I have the idea? "What if," one of us said—"what if we climbed down the pipe next to our window and snuck around to watch?"

I wasn't about to break any law myself—I didn't see sneaking out as law-breaking— but I was curious. What would happen to someone who broke a law? To someone who took a drug that movies at school had warned us about? Libby was cautious. She did not want to get into trouble. Betty and I had no qualms.

We were quiet as we began our clandestine descent down that steel pipe and tiptoed in our Keds through the soft sand to go in the front door. The downstairs was one big room, kitchen at the back and windows all around except for the enclosed staircase on our right.

Robert was in the kitchen, and when he saw our dim figures in the living room, he began hopping around, scratching under his arms like a great ape and making monkey noises. Betty and I found this hilarious but stifled our laughter—or tried to.

Our giggles added fuel to Robert's drug-addled brain, or we
were noisier than we thought, and in a few minutes the light
in the stairwell came on.

Thank goodness it was Libby. She was not so pleased.
She paused on the landing with its beaded paneling. "Please be
quieter," she said. Her frown and distressed eyes spoke
of a vivid vision of consequences if we were discovered.

We tried to quell our noise as we watched Robert's apish
behavior, but maybe his sister's appearance in the stair opening
was what sent him to a kitchen drawer. There he found a large
knife, which he whirled and threw like a knife-thrower in the
circus. At Libby. It found a target in the paneling by her head,
vibrating.

Betty and I bolted to the door. We made tracks across the
sandy yard to the steel pipe where we hauled ourselves up
to the bedroom. I had one leg over the windowsill when
Mrs. Armstrong opened our bedroom door. "What's going
on?" she said. She pretended not to notice that I was half-in,
half-outside the window.

I remember a long, six-hour bus ride back to Atlanta. Were
Betty and I cast into outer darkness because of the trouble
we'd caused the Armstrongs? Or was this the way the parents
had always planned for us to come home?

However it was, someone was in trouble. Whether it was
Betty and I for not knowing we shouldn't sneak out of upstairs

windows when we were houseguests, Libby for inviting two scofflaws to spend a week with her family, or Robert for heading down a bad road, I don't know. Maybe all of us were in trouble in one way or another. •

Nancy Tilly comes from a long line of writers and is editor of the Frasier Meadows Mirror and its upcoming literary magazine *Facets*. Nancy lives with her husband, Eben, in Boulder, Colorado, not far from son Jeb, his wife Ash and two grandsons Woods and Laz. Growing up in Atlanta, Georgia, Nancy lived 41 years in Chapel Hill, North Carolina.

Nancy's young-adult novel *The Island Summer* is available on Amazon. Based on Nancy's summer with her family on Tybee after WWII, the book follows 12-year-old Caro's adventures and friendships in a life-changing summer.

Beyond the Dark Side of the Moon
by R.V. Kuser

I had an opportunity to go to Orlando, Florida, for my senior trip in 1980. I was excited about going. We went to Disney World and SeaWorld. I had a great time. On our last day, at SeaWorld, the sky became extremely dark. There were immense and ominous clouds. This got my attention but, I figured, we are on vacation. It's all good. No big deal.

After we left SeaWorld, we went straight to the airport. About ten minutes into the flight, we hit a thunderstorm and turbulence. The motion of the plane began to resemble a Disney roller coaster ride. We were going up, down, and all around. Each time we went up, I heard, "Wow, that was great," or "Let's do it again." Then we hit a major air pocket. The plane dropped. The entire airplane became silent.

I thought, *Are we in trouble?*

The pilot came on to give us an update. He said, "We dropped approximately a thousand feet but we are stabilized now." We had a few more moments of the plane tossing around that were not severe, but what happened next was something none of us will ever forget. The flight attendant came on to make an announcement. With terror in her voice, she told us, "Put your trays back up and **please**, **please** be very careful. Don't do anything else."

At that point, I thought to myself, *We are all going to die*. It felt so surreal. I felt nauseated, anxious, and scared. I did not know what to do.

What made it even worse was that people were getting sick. The smell was quite strong. Some teachers were trying to help the students the best they could. Other teachers were in their seats, praying.

I got up to go to the bathroom. I passed a girl who was clearly scared out of her mind. She asked me to sit next to her. At that point, I could not be consoling, I was just trying to control my emotions. The best thing I could say was, "We are going to get through this okay and you'll be all right." She smiled back at me.

By this time, a lot of the people were crying, students and teachers. I went back to my seat thinking that maybe we were coming out of the worst part of the storm. Then we hit one more pocket! This one wasn't quite as severe, but I am sure it made all of us very apprehensive and scared again.

At last, the storm stopped. We were all trying to focus on getting past what just happened. Someone in my class started to listen to Pink Floyd's "The Dark Side of the Moon" on his boombox. One of the songs talks about "your head exploding with dark foreboding." The music did not make me feel happy. It seemed to illustrate what we just went through. Other people felt the same way because they said, "Can you turn the music down, please?" He then changed the album to Pink Floyd's "The Wall." That made me feel better and more relaxed. The song is about students rising up against an oppressive school. This music provided us with a sense that everything was going to be better, and we were going to get through this flight okay.

Eventually we landed safe and sound. I was grateful to be on the ground. As soon as I got off the plane, I kissed the ground. I did not know why I made that gesture, but after thinking about it now, it meant closure for me. I think the scariest part about the flight was the terror in the flight attendant's voice. When she lost it—we all started to lose it.

I have experienced anxiety at times throughout my life. It is quite troubling. My experience on that flight gave me the resolve to cope with my anxiety because it wasn't just about me. I knew I was not the only one going through the uncomfortable event. Another motivating factor was, I had just become a member of my town's fire department, which meant that I had to think of others before myself. Also, this was the first time in my life I encountered a crisis where I needed to think about other people and to rise above and beyond my own fears.

Talking and writing about the flight was a catharsis for me. Believe it or not, I have been on other flights since then. I always use coping skills. Diverting my thoughts, thinking about other people, places, or things, helps me to conquer my anxiety. •

R.V. Kuser resides in Winston Salem, North Carolina. He lives with autism. R.V. is an advocate, educator, motivational speaker, consultant and author of two books. He is on a lifelong quest for ways to overcome misperceptions about "diversely abled" individuals. To let everyone know, we CAN do anything. With his wife, Marlene, they both give a greater insight into autism when speaking publicly and advocating. They would love to hear from you—questions, comments or just to say "hello."
Contact them at kusertalk.com.

The Hazards of Democracy, 2020
by Julie Davis

B efore dawn on November 3, 2020, I drove down empty streets to a polling place in Greensboro, North Carolina. It was Election Day, and Americans were voting in the middle of a pandemic. They were deciding who among us would lead the country, our state, and local governments for the next few years while being fearful of falling ill with a mysterious new virus that had rocked the world. I had already cast my vote, taking the safest, most responsible route (in my opinion) and had voted absentee weeks ago. Instead of voting, I was there doing my civic duty another way, as a poll observer. It was in that role that I found myself pulling into the empty parking lot of a senior center on that crisp, cool fall morning. I grabbed my gear: a clipboard with instructions, phone numbers to call, a book to read during down time, snacks, a water bottle, and, of course, a mask.

The 2020 election season was a fraught time for everyone. Many voters—with competing views—were engaged and actively involved in securing votes for their preferred candidates up and down the ballot. Many pundits worried that polling places could be unruly and that voters could face intimidation and protests. Coupled with the fear of COVID-19, it was an election unlike any seen before.

Having been a poll observer in previous elections, I knew the basics. Observers watch to see if voters were being thwarted in any way. Observers mostly do just that, observe; but if a problem happens, observers can help voters cast their ballots properly. The pandemic made the whole voting process harder. Social distancing and masks were required for voters. Masks and adequate sanitizing after each voter were required for poll workers. Observers like me, from both parties, were required to be both conspicuous to voters and six feet away from other folks while wearing the ubiquitous mask.

Because options for early voting were plentiful, we never had much of a line, never more than 15 or 20 people—quite unusual for an actual election day. At times we had no one voting and no one in line. We could only guess that early voting, absentee ballots, and fear of COVID had all contributed to this smaller turnout. The room with the voting machines where we all sat to do our jobs (or in my case, observe) was not particularly big. A buzz of conversation and activity was always going on.

Then it happened. Into the room at mid-afternoon came a voter wearing a full biohazard suit. He was covered in a tan-colored jumpsuit made of stiff plastic material that crinkled when he walked. His feet were encased in black booties that came over the ankles and he wore gloves that covered his hands and wrists and pulled over his sleeves. His head was inside a weird hat that included a gas mask. His breathing was audible, and his eyes were visible through hard, clear plastic. Most concerning was the black, rectangular pouch strapped to his left leg right above the knee. It was about the size of a toaster, and it was impossible to know what it held.

All conversation throughout the room stopped when he walked in. We stopped shuffling papers, stared without flinching, and then held our collective breath to see if the trouble folks had predicted was happening to us. All other voters simply wore masks, but this one wore an entire ensemble of personal protective equipment, which could have easily hidden any number of dangers. All sorts of awful thoughts ran through my head: *Is he crazy? Does he have a gun? Does he have gas bombs? Will we survive whatever he has planned?*

We did survive, of course, and so did democracy. He voted and then crinkled his way back out to the parking lot, got into his car and drove away. When we stopped holding our individual breath, we each came to realize how important democracy is to some Americans. Silently, I applauded his sense of civic duty. He braved this strange new virus. He took the precautions he believed necessary to participate in one of America's great traditions and the one act central to our democracy: voting.

We should all take this privilege, this responsibility, as seriously as this biohazard-suit-wearing voter. The trouble is too many Americans are not as committed. I think his message to all

American citizens was loud and clear: Do whatever it takes
to cast your vote. It's your right. It's your privilege.
It's your duty. •

Julie Davis lives in Greensboro, North Carolina with her husband,
two dogs, and two cats. Writing has always been one of her hobbies.
With the exception of a piece published in *Boys' Life* magazine,
this is her first published work. She continues to write about
oddities encountered in our everyday lives.

Moonshine and Medicine

by J. Leonard Greer

Typically, Appalachia is "high-country" with government "off the mountain." Those mountain areas were ignored, and mountain people often endured a second-class citizenship and unnecessary isolation. But in that manner, they became different—and decidedly more interesting, I think. My folks, anyway.

During my youth, homemade whiskey was still valued as a medicine by many mountain people. The Great Depression was on, and doctors were scarce in many areas. Patent medicines were highly advertised, and many contained a lot of alcohol. Many mountain folks thought it not good sense to pay extra for such adulterations. Moonshine Whiskey was the ready alternative, and most families had a dependable local source. In my mother's family it was great Uncle Noah Miller.

Uncle Noah was a small operator without any desire to really cash in on the business. His still had a copper cap with a copper distillation tube called a "worm." He called this specialized equipment a "trickahmadoo." Everything else could be improvised, but this he had to have. The "trickahmadoo" was a story in itself. Once a sheriff came at night with a search warrant and the "trickahmadoo" was in the house. Noah's wife, Jenny, took it with her to bed; it was not found. She said no sheriff in the land would dare search a sick woman's bed.

Aunt Jenny helped in other ways, also. Uncle Noah was usually out somewhere on his large holding of mostly rough, mountain land. If someone came looking for him, she would go outside and yell. In the days before noise pollution, this was the usual means of local communication. Aunt Jenny's yell could differ with the occasion. If the visitor looked suspicious to her, Uncle Noah could tell by her yell and would never show up until the coast was clear.

The "trickahmadoo" was also hidden in the woods, but this was not without its problems either. Once it disappeared and was believed to have been stolen. Over a period of weeks, Uncle Noah spied on several other local operations. He found his "trickahmadoo" in use and picked his opportunity to steal it back.

One person who sometimes had use for Noah's distilled product was his sister, Frances. We called her "Aunt Francy." Aunt Francy had a pretty good education for her times. She had been sent to a boarding school when she was young. But that had not changed her outlook on how life was to be lived. She used mountain speech and kept the old ways. She always wore long skirts and did her cooking in the fireplace. She had a cook stove but used it only for canning. All this was unusual for a noted Bible scholar who could also quote some

Shakespeare if she desired. She lived alone and was remarkably self-sufficient.

Aunt Francy sometimes served as a doctor for her large family. She had several of what she called "doctor" books. She read them all but trusted some more than others. When in real doubt, she was more likely to resort to the old folk remedies. These probably did not help much but were not likely to be of harm either. Being an old maid freed her to move in and help others during a bout of sickness. I remember that she once "hallooed" our house from a nearby field. She would not come up to the house because she had been tending to Uncle Smith's family who were down with the measles. They were getting better, but she was going back to help for another spell. She was carrying her chamber pot in the crook of her arm, a bundle of clothing, and a mysterious brown jug.

Not everyone completely trusted Aunt Francy's medicine. My mother was one of these but there were others. When Uncle Noah's boys had measles, Aunt Francy treated them. Uncle Noah had measles too, but he swore everyone not to tell her, because it was said sister Francy used a sheep-dung tea as a treatment.

One might doubt Aunt Francy's medical abilities but not her faith. She was widely known and much respected as a devout Methodist. Her family had moved away from her beloved Hopewell Methodist Church years ago, but she had never found a substitute. She would walk the seven or eight miles cross-country to Hopewell services as often as she could.

She sometimes stopped at our house on the way to invite the children to go with her. Our parents were Baptist, but it would have been all right for us to go. We never did. We were afraid we could not keep up with her. She just could not wait to get there.

These stories come from a simple history of my people, and I've found there is simply no stopping place. Every question answered raises two more. And that's the trouble. •

J. Leonard Greer has lived almost 80 years in the North Carolina mountains. His ancestors were among the earliest settlers of Ashe-Watauga counties area. He never expected to write as he usually worked with his hands, but COVID-19 changed that. He had the time and felt that the family's youngsters needed to learn some family history as he had heard it from the family elders. After near 400 pages and still no stopping place in sight, it became *Oral History and My Appalachia* self-published through Cary Press. This story is an excerpt from that book.

Drownproofed

by Randell Jones

When I was a kid, I was a little intimidated by water and my ability to stay alive in it under my own power. That's why the term "drownproofing" had an appealing, if also somewhat foreboding, sound to it. But what was it exactly, other than something all students had to accomplish just to graduate from Georgia Tech?

Drownproofing was part of Swimming, one of the six "phys-ed" classes every Georgia Tech student had to take, back in the day, to get that coveted sheepskin. It had nothing to do with chemistry labs or differential equations or the mechanics of deformable bodies. It was, however, as much a rite-of-passage as passing an exam in any of those academically challenging courses. Physical education for freshmen was that twice weekly occasion when "Mother Tech" would focus all your energies so intensely on survival that you'd forget for the moment the pressures of your academic pursuits. (*Well, damn! How thoughtful.*)

The requirements to pass drownproofing were pretty straight-forward: tread water for 20 minutes with your feet tied against your waist in the lotus position; tread water for 20 minutes with your hands tied behind your back; and bob for 20 minutes in 8 feet of water with your ankles tied together and your hands tied behind your back. If you survived that, then you only had to swim 50 yards underwater in a single breath. Only.

The first week of classes could be confused because registration was still open and involved the gathering of IBM punch cards to get the classes you needed. (If you didn't live through that era of computer technology, you wouldn't believe it today, so don't ask.) The question was: would first classes actually cover anything? So, when we 150 male students showed up for Swimming for that first session, we were thinking a roll call, a course overview, and an early dismissal. The coach had other ideas.

"All right, gentlemen, we'll do swimming tests today. Meet me back here at the pool in five minutes. Be sure to take a shower. If you brought your swim trunks, wear 'em. If you didn't bring 'em, well then, boys, you'll just have to skinny dip. Let's go!"

Was he serious? Swim in the buff with 150 other buck-ass-naked guys? He was.

We shuffled off to the locker room and stripped down to the altogether. Most of our individual bodies had been deprived of sun for months. Consequently, except for the few who had swimsuits and the even fewer students-of-color who attended Tech at the time (the ridiculous Lester Maddox was then Georgia's governor), it was a pitiful, pink parade that made its way through the showers and back out into the enclosed swimming pool arena. We were in a room the size of an airplane hangar, stark naked—virtually the whole lot of us— with about a dozen doors leading directly to the outside with the possibility that at any second God-knows-who could wander right through the middle of our impromptu nudist colony.

It was awkward waiting for the coach to arrive. We had no pockets into which we could shove our hands although the automatic reflex was still there to do so. Nor could we stand there in the prominent "fig leaf" pose with our hands clasped over our privates without looking as if we were playing with ourselves. And we couldn't exactly let our hands hang idly down at our sides because we sure did not want to accidentally brush a hand or anything else against any of these other hairy, naked bodies walking around. Arms folded chest high with the hands secured in the armpits seemed to be a popular posture. Others clasped their hands behind-their-heads as if we were prisoners-of-war waiting to be marched off to some ghastly internment camp. All eyes busily inspected the ceiling.

When the coach arrived, we jumped into the pool, enveloping ourselves in the tepid pool water whose choppy surface and refractive properties offered some obscuring of our nakedness.

In the end, I did survive drownproofing and regarded it as one of the singularly most difficult achievements of my then-young life. I learned that confidence and courage are inside us. Nobody threw us in the pool tied up. We chose to jump in, acknowledging our limitations. We had to believe in ourselves to keep fear at bay and to concentrate on the task at hand—

one move, one kick, one breath at a time. That practice and that confidence got me through undergraduate engineering and two graduate degrees. It enabled me to write history, publish books, and speak before audiences around the Southeast.

And it's got me through 38 years of marriage so far. In each case, all I needed was the confidence to jump in. And I did, knowing that I was "drownproofed"—naked not required. •

Randell Jones is an award-winning writer about the pioneer and Revolutionary War eras and North Carolina history. For 13 years, he served as an invited member of the Road Scholars Speakers Bureau of the North Carolina Humanities Council. In 2013, the National Society, Daughters of the American Revolution conferred upon him its national History Award Medal. During 25 years, he has written 100+ history-based guest columns for the Winston-Salem Journal. He created the Personal Story Publishing Project and the companion podcast, "6-minute Stories" to encourage other writers. He lives in Winston-Salem, North Carolina.

www.ingramcontent.com/pod-product-compliance
Lightning Source LLC
Chambersburg PA
CBHW022020090426
42739CB00006BA/220